JB
C824
53

0 4/56 2220 JUL 2007 CH

— PEOPLE TO KNOW —

BILL COSBY

Actor and Comedian

Michael A. Schuman

Enslow Publishers, Inc.

40 Industrial Road   PO Box 38
Box 398   Aldershot
Berkeley Heights, NJ 07922   Hants GU12 6BP
USA   UK

http://www.enslow.com

> *To all those who make us laugh.*

Library of Congress Cataloging-in-Publication Data

Schuman, Michael A.
    Bill Cosby: actor and comedian / Michael A. Schuman.
        p. cm. — (People to know)
    Includes bibliographical references and index.
    Summary: Describes the life of Bill Cosby from his childhood in Philadelphia
through his successful career as a comedian.
    ISBN 0-89490-548-1
    1. Cosby, Bill, 1937– —Juvenile literature. 2. Entertainers—United
States—Biography—Juvenile literature. 3. Comedians—United States—
Biography—Juvenile Literature. [1. Cosby, Bill, 1937– . 2. Comedians.
3. Entertainers. 4. Afro-Americans—Biography.] I. Title. II. Series.
PN2287.C632S38 1995
792.7'028'092—dc20
    [B]   95-9811
                                  CIP
                                   AC

Printed in the United States of America

10 9

Illustration Credits: Children's Television Workshop, p. 66; Germantown
Historical Society, p. 19; Harvard University, p. 93; Mark Twain Archives,
Elmira College, p. 32; NBC Photo, pp. 6, 51, 55, 64, 70, 97, 99; NBC Photo
by Alan Singer, pp. 90, 95, 102; Pop Record Research, p. 47; Special
Collections and Archives, University Library, UMASS, Amherst, pp. 61, 78, 80;
Temple University, pp. 22, 24, 26, 30.

Cover Illustration: NBC Photo

Contents

Acknowledgements

Many people were of invaluable help in putting this book together, and for most, there was little if nothing in it for them. For all their time and effort I would personally like to thank: Sheldon Leonard, Dr. Alvin Poussaint, Gavin White, Paul McGuire at NBC, Ellen Turner at the *Springfield Union-News*, Al Shrier at Temple University, the staff at the Keene Public Library, the staff at the library at Keene State College, my good friend and musicologist Skip Miller, Chris Tracy at WKNE radio, my editor Damian Palisi, and the staff at Enslow Publishers.

Bill Cosby

1

A Television Pioneer

Bill Cosby was in for a surprise.

In 1964 Cosby was a young African-American comedian just starting to make a name for himself. He had appeared on television a few times and had released some comedy records that were selling well. He thought he might be able to move up in the show business world by performing on television variety shows. But he received an incredible offer: the chance to star in a major television drama series alongside an established white actor named Robert Culp.

Spy movies—especially those featuring the James Bond character—were the rage at the time. And television executives decided to take advantage of the trend by presenting a regular series about spies. Cosby and Culp's show was to be called *I Spy*. Both actors would play spies with equal intelligence and skills.

The decision to offer the role to Cosby was unusual in two ways. This type of part was usually given to a seasoned actor. Also, before 1964, no African American had ever starred in a television drama.

While it is common to see African-American actors on television today, the situation was much different in 1964. Racial segregation was legal in most of the South, where blacks—called Negroes at the time—were thought of as unfit to work as professionals or to live with whites. While there was no legal segregation in the North, many northerners felt blacks did not have the natural abilities of white people. The news that two actors—one black and one white—would work as equals in a television series made headlines across the United States.

There had been a few African Americans on television series before, but they had always been typecast in roles that were inferior to whites. They usually played maids, servants, or unskilled workers. When a famous singer named Nat "King" Cole (father of pop star Natalie Cole) hosted a television variety program in the 1950s, many southern stations refused to carry the show. As a result, Cole's show was unable to draw enough viewers to make it financially worthwhile for the network to keep it on the air. After that experience, the major networks that produce and air most television programs did not think it was worth trying another show with a black star.

That is, until a television producer and longtime actor named Sheldon Leonard came up with the idea of *I Spy* and selected Cosby to be one of the two stars. Many people in the television business as well as other observers felt southern television stations would refuse to carry *I Spy*, and the program would be a failure like Nat "King" Cole's show. Some executives at NBC-TV, the network producing the show, felt Leonard was in over his head.

At first many people at NBC thought the executives were right. When they observed Cosby in rehearsals they found that Leonard's inexperienced discovery was a poor actor. Cosby was used to telling jokes and stories on stage in front of live audiences. He seemed uncomfortable acting opposite another person, finding it hard to react to others' lines.

Leonard always had faith that Cosby would come around as a real professional. He later recalled:

> There was something charismatic about him, and the fact that when he first went before the camera he was physically awkward, not knowing where to stand and how to get there, that was a minor problem. That didn't bother me.[1]

Leonard added that he had worked with many legendary comedians who became actors, such as Bob Hope, Jack Benny, and Danny Thomas. He said that all were able to adapt to acting. Leonard stated:

> If they were any good as stand-up comics they were already getting themselves into their material and becoming a part of it, and changing their characterization to fit the material.[2]

Cosby was constantly forced to answer questions about both his ability and race. He told one reporter, "If [*I Spy*] does fail, I hope they won't say we'll never try this again with a Negro. I hope it's a case of Cosby did not come off, not a Negro did not come off."[3]

With work and coaching from both Culp and Leonard, Cosby learned to relax and show more emotion. Culp felt that Cosby was a born actor, and because of this was able to be converted from stand-up comedian to television actor in such a short time. While still critical of himself, Cosby in time became comfortable in front of a television camera.

But the battle of *I Spy* was not yet over. A large question loomed. Would southern NBC affiliates carry the show?

Thanks to the growing civil rights movement, attitudes were changing, and southern stations overwhelmingly broadcast the debut show of *I Spy* on September 15, 1965. Only four stations refused to carry it (a small number that would barely put a dent in total ratings). The four stations were in Savannah and Albany, Georgia; Birmingham, Alabama; and Daytona Beach, Florida. Around that time Cosby said:

> Without Leonard there would have been no Negro Scott. No other producer had the guts. Sure, they'd call up a Negro when they needed a slave, but this is the first time they called one up to play a spy instead of a problem.[4]

The spy show was in the top twenty for much of its first two seasons and ran until 1968 for a total of three years.

One more surprise awaited Cosby that first season. In 1965 this man, who had never acted in his life, won the Emmy Award for best lead actor in a dramatic series.

And he won the year after that, and again the year after that! In the three years *I Spy* was on the air, Cosby swept the Emmy Awards for best actor in a dramatic series.

2

Fodder for a Comedy Career

William Henry Cosby, Jr., was born in Philadelphia during the early morning hours on July 12, 1937. He was the first child of Anna and William Henry Cosby, Sr. His home was in a predominantly black section of the city called Germantown, known locally as "the Jungle." In spite of the name, there were comfortable homes in the neighborhood, and young Bill spent his first years with his parents in a modest but suitable apartment.

But while many families move to better lodgings as they grow, that was not the case with Bill's family. He later recalled, "When I was a child, we kept moving down the economic ladder."[1]

Bill's father—William Cosby, Sr.—was a welder who at first made a pretty good living. But within several years Bill's parents had three more sons. To try to escape the pressure of having to care for a larger family, William, Sr., began drinking heavily.[2] With more and more of William's wages going to alcohol, the Cosby family was forced to move twice, each time into smaller apartments in poorer neighborhoods.

One home did not even have a bathtub. The boys took baths by filling a metal tub with water, lifting it to the top of a stove for heating, then lifting it back down to the floor and climbing inside it. Ultimately, the Cosby family settled in a first floor apartment in a complex called the Richard Allen Homes, also known as "the projects." The apartments were in the shadow of frequently-used train tracks. Cosby recalled, "There was a railroad bridge and when Mother would hang clothes the trains would go by and dirty them. But it wasn't a life of poverty. We always had plenty of hot water and heat."[3]

By now, Bill's father was spending more time in neighborhood bars and less time at home.[4] Bill had a younger brother named James, who had been a sickly child. When James was six years old he died of rheumatic fever (an illness causing permanent damage to the heart). That tragedy seemed to be the final blow for William Cosby, Sr. He left his family and joined the Navy.

At eleven years old, Bill was now the oldest male in the household. His father sent money home now and then to help support his family, but the amount was never sufficient. Bill became the "man of the house." So in addition to attending school, he worked several odd jobs. Bill spent mornings before school either shining shoes on a makeshift box that he had made or selling fruit at a neighborhood market. After school he had to take care of his two surviving younger brothers, Russell and Robert, until his mother came home from her job. Anna worked as a housekeeper, cleaning other people's homes. She often worked up to twelve hours a day.

At times the Cosby family had to rely on welfare, but mostly they got by. They paid the rent and grocery bills with money Anna, Bill, or even the two young boys, had earned. However, Anna's priorities were always her children. Bill later remembered how at the end of a long work day she sometimes went without eating. She gave her supper to one of Bill's growing brothers who was still hungry after he had finished his own meal.

When things looked bad, Bill's mother responded with tears. If Bill fought with his brothers or broke a household appliance while playing recklessly, Anna would cry. Watching her, the boys would behave. Bill later said, "Her tears alone would shake us up. She'd start crying and you'd start crying."[5] Cosby also related how the fear of his mother's tears kept him from getting into trouble on the streets. He said:

> The thing that always turned me around and kept me from taking a pistol and holding up a store or jumping in and beating some old person on the street was that I could go to jail, and this would bring a great amount of shame on my mother...."[6]

14

But even the thought of his mother's teary eyes couldn't turn young Bill Cosby into a good student—in spite of Anna Cosby's strong emphasis on education. Anna often read to Bill and his brothers, especially the Bible and the works of Mark Twain.

While Twain's depictions of African Americans might be considered racist by today's standards, in his day he was well ahead of his time. Twain was one of the first white American authors to depict blacks as human beings with feelings. It was Twain's humor that helped influence Cosby's comic routines. In fact, in the late 1960s some referred to Cosby as "an electronic Mark Twain."[7]

But in school, Bill was more interested in playing the class clown than in being the scholar. And in the inner city school system Bill was part of, many teachers had long given up on their students.

One exception was Mary Forchic, an elementary school teacher of Bill's who took a special interest in each of her pupils. She looked for a special talent each might have, and she made efforts to encourage students by buying them treats or gifts when they achieved something noteworthy.

Noticing Bill's pleasure in entertaining his classmates with his jokes and funny actions, Miss Forchic once scolded him with a statement that turned out to be prophetic. She said, "In this classroom there is one comedian and it is I. If you want to be one, grow up, get your own stage, and get paid for it."[8]

But at the same time Miss Forchic recognized that Bill had a talent for performing. Making his classmates happy with his actions was the equivalent of being loved and appreciated.[9]

So Miss Forchic cast him in several school plays. It is hard to believe now that one of the first performances of his long and distinguished career would be a starring role in a play titled *King Koko from Kookoo Island.*

Bill graduated from one grade to the next, but his marks were consistently poor, or at best, mediocre. His main interest, aside from joking around, was sports. In junior high school he was named captain of his school's tumbling team.

Still, some of his teachers realized that he had great potential and an IQ test proved that they were right. (The letters *IQ* stand for "intelligence quotient," and the test is meant to determine a person's natural mental skills and reasoning ability.) Cosby's score on the IQ test ranked near the top.

As a result of the test, along with good recommendations from his teachers, Bill, now a teenager, was given a rare privilege. He was allowed to attend a special boys-only public school in Philadelphia called Central High School. The school was for highly intelligent, or what were called "gifted," students. It had up-to-date facilities and an ambitious student body—the vast majority of whom went on to college.

Central High also had a football team with handsome uniforms, which drew Bill's attention like a magnet. He had been used to street football, dodging cars and manhole covers on the pavement in his neighborhood. Bill had thought of sports as a way out of the inner city. But his dreams were over in a flash. Bill broke his arm in the first week of practice.

The quality of Central High's academics had no effect on Bill's grades, however. If anything, the special school's atmosphere made it tougher on this sophomore from the projects. Many of the students were from wealthy neighborhoods and were taking advanced courses. Bill did not fit in, nor did he have the background to readily adjust to this new environment.

He continued to play the class clown to both students and teachers. Once a teacher caught him reading a comic book in class and grabbed it away from him, saying, "You'll get this back at the end of the school year."

"Why?" Bill responded. "Does it take you that long to read it?"[10]

Bill's sophomore year was a disaster, and he was forced to repeat his courses the next year. Unused to being held back and still uncomfortable with this special school, Bill transferred back to his neighborhood public high school, Germantown High.

Bill adapted fairly well once he was back in his old neighborhood. He made both the football and track teams and was chosen captain of each. He also enjoyed the company of female students, something lacking at the all-male Central High School. Bill plodded along academically, but at age nineteen he still had not graduated. Discouraged and in want of money, Cosby dropped out of high school in 1956.

Cosby took a few odd jobs such as working in a muffler shop and a shoe repair store. But he realized there was no future in his situation. In search of stability and steady earnings, Cosby followed the example set by his father and enlisted in the U.S. Navy.

As far as timing, Cosby was lucky since America was between wars. The Korean War ended in 1953 and America would not be sending troops to Vietnam for several years. So Cosby served peacetime duty and learned the skills to be a physical therapist, helping disabled veterans regain basic skills such as eating and walking by themselves. In the Navy he traveled to such places as Canada, Cuba, and Argentina. Most of the time, though, he was stationed stateside. Bill spent time at Quantico, a Marine base in Virginia, and at Bethesda Naval Hospital in Maryland.

Cosby became a competent physical therapist. He not only learned the basic skills, but also enjoyed cracking jokes and making his patients laugh, which lifted the spirits of the physically injured men. But the idea of a career in the Navy with all the required discipline and obedience to senior officers did not appeal to him.[11]

Germantown High, where Bill Cosby attended high school until dropping out at the age of nineteen.

Still, his four-year tenure in the service did more for Cosby than enable him to learn a skill. He later admitted that the discipline helped him develop maturity and self-reliance. He remembered:

> In boot camp, the force and the discipline were devastating to me. For the first time, I wasn't able to argue or make an excuse for why I did not do something.[12]

Cosby also earned a spot on the Navy track team, excelling in the high jump and winning several awards. More importantly, he grew up during this period and learned some valuable lessons. He later said:

> I met a lot of guys in the Navy who didn't have as much upstairs as I knew I did, yet here they were struggling away for an education. I finally realized I was committing a sin—a mental sin.[13]

With that in mind, Cosby studied and took a test that would give him the equivalent of a high school diploma. When his term of service was up at age twenty-three he felt he was too old to live back at home and had too much intelligence and athletic ability to waste. He decided to go to college.

3

The Funnyman in the Cellar

Bill Cosby was no longer the wise guy kid who spent more time in school making jokes than taking notes. This time he was serious about getting an education. He was well aware that without an education, his career choices would be limited.

Low on money, Cosby realized it would be practical for him to stay close to Philadelphia. There he could temporarily live at home with his mother to save on room and board expenses. Temple University, a major university near Cosby's home in north Philadelphia, was willing to take a chance on the ex-serviceman. Because Cosby had demonstrated his athletic skills to Temple's coaches, he was awarded a full tuition scholarship in track and field.

As in the Navy, the high jump was Cosby's best event—although he was an all-around skilled track

Bill Cosby was awarded a full tuition scholarship in track and field at Temple University.

athlete who competed in as many as six events. He also played fullback on Temple's football team. But his former track and freshman football coach, Gavin White, says that track was definitely his better sport.[1]

Because of the four years he had spent in the Navy, a career as a professional athlete was unlikely. Cosby entered college as a freshman at age twenty-three. Most other freshmen were eighteen years old and right out of high school. After attending four years of college he would be twenty-seven, which is late to think about starting a professional sports career.

So Cosby majored in physical education with plans to teach after graduation. He liked campus life and spent the little leisure time he had playing the drums, making friends, and dating. Unlike his days in public school, Cosby managed to keep his grades up too. He did quite well, Gavin White remembered:

> In fact, he made the dean's list and he joked about that. He said he came to the stadium one day and he wanted to find out from the other kids what the dean's list meant. He had no academic background and he never made any special list academically. He thought maybe it meant that he was thrown out of school. Making the dean's list meant that he had at least a 3.0 average, which is quite good. It's above a B average, which shows you just what kind of a student he was.[2]

This is not to say that Cosby suddenly lost his sense of humor and his passion for clowning around. White

Bill Cosby, a gifted athlete, played fullback on Temple University's football team.

recalled times when Cosby turned football and track team meetings into comedy sessions, making him the most popular team member as well as the oldest.

White said, "He was always funny. He'd do takeoffs on the coaches, giving his impression of what the coaches were saying that day but in his own inimitable style."[3]

One of what Gavin White called "Cosby's funniest nights" was at a special ceremony after a practice at Temple University Stadium. New lights had just been installed and the local press was invited to cover the event. Prior to the ceremony, Ernie Casale, Temple's athletic director, addressed the athletes. He ordered them to stay on hand for the entire event, even though most were hungry after their workout and simply wished to leave and get something to eat.

Cosby then followed Casale's speech with a satirical imitation of it. White recalled:

> Bill stood up before the players and gave this speech mimicking Mr. Casale, saying things like, 'If you fellows would like to leave, it's perfectly all right.' But then he would remind the kids in the same breath that if they left the stadium there were seven guys outside with sub-machine guns waiting for them. In other words, you must be there for the lighting ceremony. It was ridiculous but he'd do it in such a way that it sounded almost real.[4]

It was not long before Cosby used his sense of humor and quick wit to make a little money on the side.

Temple University track coach Gavin White, Jr., was an important person in Bill Cosby's life.

But his introduction into show business came about accidentally.

Like many students, Cosby needed pocket money to pay for books, living expenses, and entertainment. He took odd jobs, including working as a lifeguard at a Philadelphia swimming pool. During the summer following his freshman year, he traveled to California with plans to see the country and pick up some summer work. However, Cosby was not successful in finding employment, something he blames on racism.[5]

Cosby stayed home in Philadelphia following the completion of his sophomore year. He had a friend who owned a small bar called The Underground, which was located in the cramped basement of a building. His friend got Cosby a job tending bar there, mixing alcoholic drinks for the patrons. But like many bartenders, there was a secondary part of his job—making conversation with and being friendly to the customers.

Cosby knew that the more entertaining he was and the more he could make the customers laugh, the larger his tips would be. The bar owner noticed the way Cosby would add a dash of humor to his drinks and how the customers seemed to love it. He offered Cosby a job telling jokes to the people as they sat at tables, nursing their drinks. Though Cosby never had any plans to get into show business, he accepted the job.

Word started filtering through the local community that there was a very funny bartender telling jokes at The Underground. With more people coming to see Cosby, the owner of the bar moved his star comedian to a nightclub called The Cellar in another part of the same building. Here Cosby was given more time to tell his jokes.

The Cellar had no stage, and like The Underground, The Cellar was small. It was so small, in fact, that the six-foot-tall Cosby was unable to stand straight without hitting his head on the ceiling. So he sat on a chair that had been placed atop a table. From his perch, Cosby told humorous stories about college life or experiences on the football or track teams.

At the time that Cosby was charming audiences in The Cellar, it was common for nationally-known comedians to release their routines on record albums. Today, with many outlets for comedians—such as videotapes and abundant cable channels—this is rare. In the early 1960s, however, records gave comedians exposure that they could never have received from only live performances. With records, their routines could be heard both on radio and on people's stereos in their homes.

College students, especially, were buying and playing comedy records. So Cosby began to broaden his routines, adding jokes that he had heard told by then popular young comedians such as Jonathan Winters,

Mort Sahl, Shelley Berman, and Bob Newhart. For the most part, these comedians' material consisted of cutting edge social satire, offbeat interpretations of then popular politicians, or their views of much-studied philosophers.

Cosby would listen carefully to their performances. He would study their timing (the rhythm in which they told their jokes) and their deliveries (the manner in which they said the words). Through practice and listening to others, Cosby began to perfect his own individual style.

All this time Cosby was still a student at Temple University. He continued to attend classes and study as well as compete in track meets. But he also wanted to continue to take advantage of his comic abilities. By making contacts he was able to get himself booked, or hired, to perform in more Philadelphia-area clubs.

Many of the clubs were low-class burlesque houses in which Cosby was hired mainly to fill time between strippers' acts. The audiences were not interested in hearing a comedian doing satirical or political humor. He was often ignored by his audiences or fired by his bosses. Young entertainers just starting out, however, cannot afford to take any kind of exposure for granted, and Cosby would not turn down any opportunity to work.

There were nightclub owners who asked Cosby to spice up his act by telling dirty jokes, swearing occasionally for shock value, or making comments about sex for easy laughs. But he refused. Cosby, simply, was

Even while performing in The Cellar, Cosby remained a student at Temple University. Shown here is the Bell Tower, a central meeting place on the main campus.

too clever a comedian to resort to cheap humor. The key for Cosby was to entertain people by using his natural creativity.

Others wanted Cosby to emphasize racial humor. Dick Gregory, a popular comedian who later became an activist and alternative nutritional counselor, used this kind of humor. The civil rights movement was gaining steam in the United States, and jokes about the movement and the differences between the races were popular—especially among blacks and white liberals.

But this was not Cosby's style either, although he did resort to racial humor on occasion—especially if he felt that an audience was otherwise unreceptive to his typical routines. Racial jokes served to reach an otherwise passive crowd by shocking them, but without having to resort to vulgarity.

"You better laugh," he would say now and then. "I have a club that's the opposite of the Ku Klux Klan."[6]

Ultimately, Cosby discovered what would be his most fruitful source for inspiration: his childhood. He recalled how his mother read the Bible and works by Mark Twain, and he remembered his neighborhood friends. Cosby realized he did not have to parrot other comedians or borrow their material when he had such a fountainhead of ideas in his past. In fact, he combined Mark Twain's understanding of human nature with a famous Bible story to create what became one of his most famous routines.

Bill Cosby combined Mark Twain's (shown here) understanding of human nature with his own comedic talent to create some of his most famous routines.

But before he perfected that routine, he felt he needed greater exposure. The most promising young comedians were working in an area called Greenwich Village in New York City, less than a two-hour train ride from Philadelphia. In the late 1950s and early 1960s, Greenwich Village attracted young people whose interests in art and lifestyles tended to be unconventional.

Cosby felt his wry humor would have a receptive audience in Greenwich Village. And in the spring of 1962, Bill Cosby—college student, track star, and budding comedian—set off for New York.

4

College Comedian

Cosby auditioned at several New York nightclubs and coffeehouses before Clarence Hood, a white man originally from the South, hired the young black comic to work at his place. It was a well-known coffeehouse in Greenwich Village called The Gaslight. (Coffeehouses are nightclubs where coffee is served and entertainment is often provided. They were very popular at the time.)

Cosby said, "The boss at The Gaslight offered me $60 a week, and I was thrilled to death. Then I realized that out of that $60 a week I had to pay for a place to stay." He was referring to the nights he would not be driving back to Philadelphia. Cosby continued:

> The boss offered to let me sleep in the upstairs storeroom. All it had was a cot. No bathroom. But he gave me a key to the club so I could go downstairs and clean up before the public came in. It kinda reminded me of the Navy, sleeping on that cot.[1]

Still a student at Temple, Cosby did have to travel back to Philadelphia often in order to keep up his studies. He arranged his work schedule so that he could be in class during the day and on stage in Greenwich Village at night. It was an exhausting pace.

About this time, Cosby was perfecting his "Noah's Ark" routine, which would become his first classic act. In it, Cosby interprets how a modern man would react if he heard the voice of God in the same way Noah did. Cosby started the routine with God calling out to Noah:

"Noah!"

Cosby, as Noah, looks up. "Who is that?"

"It's the Lord, Noah."

Noah responds sarcastically, "Ri-ight."

God instructs Noah, "I want you to build an ark."

Noah answers, "Ri-ight." Then he pauses, before continuing. "What's an ark?"

God instructs him. "Get some wood. Build it Three Hundred cubits by Eighty cubits by Forty cubits." (These are the same measurements for an ark as those in Genesis, the first book in the Bible.)

Noah replies, "Ri-ight. What's a cubit?"

God tells Noah he is planning to destroy the world.

Noah questions the Lord, "Am I on *Candid Camera?*" (*Candid Camera* was a television show in the 1950s and 1960s in which average people were unknowingly filmed while placed in strange situations.)

God persists, "I'm going to make it rain 4,000 days and drown them right out."

And Noah says, "Ri-ight. Let it rain for 40 days and 40 nights and wait for the sewers to back up."

And God responds in language he thinks Noah will understand, "RI-IGHT!"

Noah is convinced. He builds the ark while his neighbors laugh at him, thinking he is crazy. After the ark is completed the rain comes down in torrents.

Noah is convinced. He looks up and says, "Okay, Lord. Me and you. Right."[2]

At times, Cosby did resort to the racial humor that he disliked. After all, he was just starting out, and racial humor was topical as well as popular with audiences.

A few months after his debut at The Gaslight, summer arrived, which meant no classes to complicate his schedule or to pull his attention away from his comedy jobs. Cosby was given an extended contract at The Gaslight and an increased salary of $175 a week. It would ultimately rise to $200 a week, an exorbitant amount for the time.

Early that summer *The New York Times* gave Cosby a rave review, even though the article put the emphasis on the racial humor Cosby put into his act. The headline read, "Comic Turns Quips Into Tuition." And the lead paragraph began:

> The Gaslight Cafe, a subterranean coffee house in Greenwich Village, is featuring a young Negro

comic who is working his way through college by hurling verbal spears at the relations between whites and Negroes.

The review brought attention to Cosby's athletic talents, noting:

> Besides verbal spears Mr. Cosby throws the discus, the javelin, broad jumps, high jumps, runs the 220-low hurdles and plays right halfback on Temple's football team.

The reviewer said that seeing Cosby was well worth the trip into Greenwich Village:

> Mr. Cosby writes his own material. Although his output thus far is limited, his viewpoint is fresh, slightly ironic, and his best quips are extremely funny. He is a man of considerable promise who should keep Gaslight habitues laughing between sips of expresso. . . several leading comics may have sleepless nights this fall."[3]

This review brought hordes of curious people to hear Cosby on stage, increasing his marketability. He was booked to work clubs in other large cities such as Chicago and Washington, D.C. And he was building a reputation in the entertainment business. Of course, like any artist or performer just starting out, there were weeks in which Cosby could not get work and had no money coming in. But overall, life was on the upswing.

With the coming of fall, Cosby registered for classes for his junior year at Temple, planning to continue both his studies and his comedy career. But inevitably a conflict between the two arose.

Without the time to concentrate on his studies, combined with a transient lifestyle, Cosby's grades began to slip. He also had difficulty staying in shape. Finally the situation came to a head one fall weekend. Cosby was offered $250 to perform on a Friday night in Philadelphia's Town Hall—the same night the football team was to travel to Toledo, Ohio, (550 miles away) to prepare for a Saturday game.

Not wanting to turn down an income-producing and prestige-building performance, Cosby asked for a favor. He wanted to fly to Toledo on his own on Saturday, arriving in time for the game. His request was denied. There would be no special rules for any one player.

That led to a greater problem. If Cosby did not travel with the team and play by the school's rules, he would be dropped from the team. And if he was dropped from the team, he would lose his athletic scholarship.

Cosby made a difficult choice. He quit college, just as he had left high school six years before. This time, however, he had a real dream to follow. Cosby's former coach Gavin White remembered the day Cosby left college:

> He felt obligated to me because I had given him the scholarship and I had been the one to bring him there. Even though he was playing football he

was at Temple on a track scholarship. So he came into my office and told me how sorry he felt about leaving because he had done well in his initial track season and he knew I was counting on him.

But he explained what he wanted to do and that he thought he could make out well in comedy. So I wished him luck and the only thing I ever told Bill was, "Look. No matter where you go or what you do, stay in shape. Always try to take care of your body." Of course, he followed that faithfully. That's why he became interested in tennis, and later running, and so forth.[4]

The fact that Cosby was embarking on a second career as a comedian was no surprise to the Temple coaching staff. Gavin White admits he had heard about Cosby's on-stage performances from Cosby's teammates, and after all, it was hard to keep something like that a secret. Many of Cosby's teammates were his best customers.

White remembered, "I think Bill was a little reluctant to tell me. I guess he was afraid of what my interpretation might have been, but it didn't bother me really."[5] When asked what he thought of Cosby's decision at the time White replied:

He was an intelligent kid so I knew he had the ability to make decisions that were right for him. And of course, I had seen the comedy side of him at camps and in different ways. So I felt he had a good chance for success. And then some of the kids used to tell me about his appearances at some of the clubs and how funny he was.

39

I didn't try to talk him out of it. I can't say I was convinced he was going to make it in that medium. Nobody could have said that. But I wasn't surprised by it either.[6]

One person did try to talk him out of it—his mother. Anna Cosby felt that he was throwing away an education, a career, and a financially secure future. Having placed so much importance on getting an education, she felt her son should stay the last year and a half and finish college, believing he would never get another chance.[7]

But Cosby's career was starting to steamroll. He hired a manager named Roy Silver, who had seen Cosby perform and liked what he saw. And he was getting bookings all over North America, in well-known nightclubs in Washington, D.C., San Francisco, and Toronto. Cosby's earnings increased as he became better known and started to reach larger audiences.

Silver and Cosby would spend days analyzing the comic's performances, timing, and material, and helping him polish his stage presence. Silver also gave Cosby the confidence he needed to succeed. He saw Cosby as a man with the ability to become a big name headliner and star. With Silver's support, Cosby began to look at himself in the same manner.[8]

By now Cosby was giving his routines a new angle. He veered away from racial humor for good, stating, "Rather than trying to bring the races of people together by talking about the differences, let's try and bring them together by talking about the similarities."[9]

That he did. Reaching back into his childhood memories, Cosby talked about the youngsters in his neighborhood such as Fat Albert, Weird Harold, and Dumb Donald as well as the experiences he had growing up. Though members of his audience might not have grown up in the inner city of Philadelphia, they related to what he said. Cosby knew that some feelings and situations are universal, experienced by all people growing up, regardless of their race, ethnic background, or residency.

Cosby joked about playing football in the street, dodging cars to catch the ball. He even exaggerated about a teammate hopping aboard a bus to make a catch. He told amusing tales about believing that monsters were living in his bedroom closet when he was a child. His mother would come in when Bill called and pretend to chase the monsters away, while his father would just say, "Okay. Let them eat you up."[10]

Or he would talk about the times the gang had slushball fights with each other in winter, or an occasion when he fought over the limited space in the bedroom he shared with his little brother.

One time when he was performing in Washington, D.C., a friend tried to plan a blind date with a woman named Camille Hanks. She was a nineteen-year-old psychology student at the University of Maryland.

Hanks was very attractive and from a much different background than Cosby.

Her father was a research chemist at Walter Reed Hospital, a major army hospital in Washington, D.C. Her mother was director of a nursery school. She grew up in the comfortable suburb of Silver Spring, Maryland, in a spacious neighborhood far different than the streets of inner city Philadelphia.

At first, she wanted nothing to do with this guy named Bill Cosby. She had not met him but had heard he was a college dropout trying to make a career in show business. Her parents thought little of entertainment personalities and those feelings trickled down to their daughter.

But Cosby was persistent, and ultimately, Hanks decided to go out with him. They enjoyed each other's company and continued dating. In just three months they were engaged.

The engagement did not last long. Hanks's parents forced her to call it off. They felt Cosby, like most struggling performers, faced an uncertain future and they believed his business was populated by people who were irresponsible and had low morals. In brief, they thought he was just not good enough for their daughter.[11]

Cosby continued to see Hanks in spite of the broken engagement. In one day he would drive two hundred miles from New York to Maryland, take Hanks to lunch or a matinee movie, then drive back to New York in order to perform that night. This relationship continued for several months until they became engaged again. Camille's parents still were not pleased with the idea of their daughter marrying this young comedian. But they accepted the fact that Camille and Bill were in love and they refused to interfere.

5

On to the Small Screen

Cosby had gotten his first national exposure when he and
Camille were dating. While he had become a big star in
night clubs, the fact was then as it is now, that millions
more people watch television than go to night clubs. The
publicity from a mass medium such as television can offer a
considerable boost to an entertainer's career that would be
impossible in night clubs alone.

He certainly tried to get the needed exposure,
auditioning on several occasions for NBC's *The Tonight
Show*, which was then hosted by Johnny Carson and
taped live in New York City. But all Cosby got was
rejection after rejection. When he was given the chance
to make his television debut on *The Tonight Show*, it was
only because the host, Johnny Carson, decided to take a
vacation.

The show still went on even when Carson was away. Chosen to substitute for Carson that night was a well-known comedian named Allan Sherman. Sherman was famous for his record albums satirizing popular and classical songs. He would create new and funny lyrics to well-known songs in the same manner that Weird Al Yankovic does today.

In the summer of 1963 Sherman became a household name when he had a hit comedy single. It was to the tune of a classical composition called "Dance of the Hours," which an Italian composer named Amilcare Ponchielli wrote in the nineteenth century. To this day when people attending a concert hear Ponchielli's work performed, many are still reminded of Sherman's satirical words.

Sherman called it, "Hello Muddah, Hello Fadduh! (A Letter From Camp)" and humorously told the story about a homesick boy writing to his parents, begging to come home. What made it funny was the boy's exaggerations. He said that other boys were disappearing or being poisoned, and that "The food here is improving. The little black things in it aren't moving."[1]

People could relate to the youthful overstatements Sherman employed in the song in the same manner that they related to Bill Cosby's funny and overstated tales of youth. Perhaps Sherman saw some of himself in Cosby and in some of the material Cosby created.

Sherman called Cosby to come and audition, but Cosby was so discouraged by his repeated rejections that he almost did not show up.[2] When Cosby did arrive at the NBC studios, Sherman asked him to demonstrate what he would do on stage if given the chance. Cosby did not do his Noah's Ark routine, something he had by now perfected thanks to practice and numerous performances. And he did not do jokes about his childhood.

Instead he did a different routine that had received laughs in New York nightclubs. In this one he satirized followers and students of karate, a martial art that was a fad at the time. He joked about graduates of karate schools who felt invincible after taking a brief course. And he made fun of the required but highly dramatic yell that accompanied a karate chop.

The audience at *The Tonight Show* loved Cosby's performance. Sherman was so impressed that when Cosby, along with Cosby's manager Roy Silver, released his first record album later in 1963, Sherman helped produce it. The record was called *Bill Cosby Is a Very Funny Fellow . . . Right!*, and consisted of Cosby's live performance at a nightclub called The Bitter End in Greenwich Village.

Sherman also wrote the liner notes (the words on the back of the jacket the record was packaged in). He raved about Cosby's Noah's Ark routine, calling it a "masterpiece." He elaborated:

> It's warm, and human, and honest, and deeply moving, and it's funny. It's going to be a classic. . . .

46

Allan Sherman became a household name in the summer of 1963. After appearing with Sherman on *The Tonight Show*, Cosby's first album was made with Sherman's help.

Bill Cosby, if I am any judge of talent, will keep coming up with fresh, new material and will grow everyday in stature and importance on the American comedy scene.[3]

His prediction was accurate.

In regards to Cosby's race, Sherman made it clear that people knew it was talent, not race, that made Cosby funny. Sherman said:

Bill Cosby would be funny if he were green or purple or chartreuse. He's funny because he can feel for people—and he can communicate that feeling. . . . I'm so proud and happy for the chance to introduce you to Bill Cosby. It isn't every day that we come in contact with greatness. The day you first listen to this album will be one of those days for you.[4]

While Sherman lived to see Cosby's success in *I Spy*, he unfortunately would not be around to see him reach legendary proportions with *The Cosby Show*. Sherman died prematurely at the age of forty-eight in 1973.

On the album were Cosby's early routines, including the ones about karate and Noah's ark. He also joked about the strange people who ride New York City subways, television commercials featuring endorsements by athletes, and the way women seem to go to public restrooms in numbers. Surprisingly, there was no material about growing up.

The recording sold reasonably well, and Cosby was nominated for a Grammy award in 1963 for best comedy album. In a touch of irony, he lost to a record by Allan Sherman.

On January 25, 1964, Bill Cosby and Camille Hanks were married in the town of Olney, Maryland. It is typical in show business for entertainers to perform on holidays or important days in their personal lives. So it was not unusual that Bill had to do a show the night of his wedding. Camille spent her wedding night watching her husband on stage.

Immediately afterward they flew to San Francisco, where Cosby did another show at a nightclub called the Hungry i. Then they traveled to Los Angeles where Bill was scheduled to perform at yet another club, the Crescendo. And they went on to Lake Tahoe, a resort in Nevada, where Cosby had another date at Harrah's, a famous casino and club. The couple had a highly unusual honeymoon!

Cosby's second album *I Started Out as a Child,* which contained many of his trademark childhood stories, came out in 1964. Again Cosby was nominated for a Grammy, and this time, he won.

On the album were his stories about playing street football and one about the first boy in his neighborhood to own a pair of sneakers. Cosby introduced his fans to his family on this record, including his brothers, his mother, and his father—whom he referred to as "the Giant," a man more feared than respected. He also used other themes, such as a story about The Wolfman—the subject of a famous horror movie—going into a barber shop for a haircut. And he talked about some of the silly comments well-meaning people say at funerals.

Cosby's first two albums were not best-sellers, but they did show respectable numbers at music store cash registers. They also earned critical praise, including the one Grammy award. However, his third album *Why Is There Air?* was a huge hit. Released in 1965, it won Cosby another Grammy for best comedy album.

Just before *Why Is There Air?* was released, the *I Spy* pilot (the first episode) was given a go-ahead. Television producer Sheldon Leonard felt all along that Cosby would be perfect for the role of Alexander Scott, a spy who masqueraded as the trainer for a tennis star named Kelly Robinson, who was actually another spy played by Robert Culp. Leonard said he first became acquainted with Cosby after seeing him perform on a special hosted by Jack Paar, a popular television personality in the early 1960s.

In 1965, Leonard was a veteran movie actor and producer in his late fifties. In the movies he usually played a tough guy or gangster. Every Christmas you can see him on television in the classic movie, *It's a Wonderful Life.* He plays Nick, the bartender.

But as a television producer in the 1950s he developed family situation comedies. His best known were *The Danny Thomas Show, The Andy Griffith Show,* and *The Dick Van Dyke Show.* All three shows are viewed

Television producer Sheldon Leonard felt all along that Cosby would be perfect for a leading role in *I Spy*.

today as classics from the early days of television, and reruns of the shows are still shown.

Years later Leonard said that he felt audiences in 1965 were ready to accept an African American in a lead role on television. As proof he offered mail that he had received over the previous ten years as he gradually introduced African-American actors into his television shows.

The cast of *The Danny Thomas Show* in the 1950s included a black supporting actress named Amanda Randolph. If Thomas, a white man, ever kissed Randolph on the cheek or put his arm around her, Leonard recollected:

> I could be sure I'd get buckets of mail protesting, saying things like, "Whenever I want to see a white man making love to a gorilla I'll go to a freak show," things like that. I might get six or seven or eight postcards, all signed with different names, but all having the same handwriting with the same postmark, as each of these bigoted idiots tried to make themselves seem like more than they were. And I saved all that mail.[5]

In the early 1960s Leonard produced what would be a landmark episode on *The Dick Van Dyke Show*. In the show Van Dyke played a New York writer named Rob Petrie. In this particular episode Rob was worried that the newborn baby he and his wife had just taken home from the hospital was not theirs. He was convinced that his baby had been switched with a newborn baby that belonged to a couple who stayed in a nearby room and was delivered the same day. The two couples had similar names—the other couple was named Peters. Even though Rob had never actually seen or met the other couple, he was sure the name similarity was the reason for the mix-up.

So Van Dyke called the other couple and invited them to his house to discuss the matter. As soon as Van Dyke opened the door to greet them, he knew their babies could not have been switched. The other couple was black, and Van Dyke had made a big fool of himself.

While today's audiences would not be the slightest bit shocked at such a scene, this was a very touchy and controversial topic to address in the early 1960s. Issues of race were viewed as too sensitive to be topics of situation comedies. The possibility that conservative whites would be offended was great. Yet Leonard had the courage to do it. Years later Leonard said:

> I got mail after that episode, too. But it was of an entirely different complexion than the Amanda Randolph mail. It was kind of congratulatory. People said it was so nice to see a black man one-upping a white man and being treated with dignity and as a cultured and intelligent and an attractive person.[6]

The times were changing. Leonard felt that American audiences were ready for *I Spy* and Bill Cosby.

But Leonard still had to convince NBC's president Bob Kintner, and he was concerned about Kintner's reaction.[7] As it turned out, he did not have to be. Kintner was receptive to the idea of Cosby as Culp's co-star. To this day Leonard gives Kintner credit for breaking the color barrier on television:

> The entrance of Cosby into television was the result of the courage and the open mindedness of one man. That was Bob Kintner . . . the door came wide open and in the next year or two there was a positive flood of black actors and black shows on the air.[8]

Leonard said that he was not surprised that only four southern stations did not air the first episode of *I Spy*, although many network executives were. They feared another southern boycott, like the one that occurred nine years earlier regarding Nat "King" Cole's show.[9]

He also stated that he was never truly concerned about Cosby's acting ability, even though it has been reported that he was. But Leonard did give much credit to co-star Robert Culp in helping Cosby make the adjustment into acting. Leonard said:

> When I made the pilot for *I Spy* the network people were very frightened of Cosby. They tried to persuade me to recast the part. But on the basis of my own experience with stand-up comics I knew that he needed a brief transition period and he'd be all right. So I said, "If he goes, I go, too," and that put an end to that.[10]

Bill Cosby starred with Robert Culp in the detective series, *I Spy*.

Of course, Leonard's feelings were right. Cosby won Emmy awards and the show won ratings. Life was going well at home too. Cosby and Camille's first child, a daughter named Erika, was born on April 8, 1965. Their second daughter, Erinn, was born just over a year later.

(The Cosby's were starting a trend with their children's names. All five of their children's names would start with the letter *E*, which Cosby said stands for "excellence.")

Unfortunately, Cosby was on location filming *I Spy* in Hong Kong when his first child was born. Unlike the vast majority of television shows, *I Spy* was not filmed in studios or on sound stages. Instead it was filmed in exotic locations around the world. But Cosby was able to be at home to share in the birth of his and Camille's second child.

Sheldon Leonard's contract to produce *I Spy* expired in 1968 and he did not try to renew it. NBC had moved the hit program from Wednesday night at 10:00 P.M. to Monday at 9:00 P.M. for its third season. The ratings decreased, and some critics theorized that this was because the spy fad had run its course. Others felt that with the unpopular war in Vietnam raging, television viewers had trouble putting their faith in government spies, even if they were fictional. Leonard said that none of this was true. The low ratings were strictly caused by the bad time slot and economics:

> They approached me about a pick-up for a fourth year but I didn't accept it because in the time spot they had given me I could see nothing but

diminishing value for the show in terms of resale or syndication. The very seriously depleted ratings wouldn't do me any good.[11]

For Cosby it did not matter. His reputation was solid. He was now doing stand-up comedy shows in major clubs and making up to $40,000 a week. He continued to release comedy record albums such as *Wonderfulness* in 1966, *Revenge* in 1967, and *To Russell, My Brother Whom I Slept With* in 1968. In 1969, after the run of *I Spy* ended, he released another comedy album, titled *Sports*. He won Grammy awards for each of the four recordings.

He also released, in 1968, the first of several music albums he would record over the years. Cosby sang live in nightclubs such as the Whisky a Go-Go in Los Angeles, and mockingly referred to himself as Silver Throat. His first album was called *Bill Cosby Sings/ "Silver Throat."* It featured a hit single titled, "Little Old Man," a half-spoken, half-sung tune he co-wrote with Stevie Wonder. In 1967 it peaked at No. 4 on the charts of *Billboard Magazine*, the trade magazine for the recording industry.[12]

During his early years Cosby had thoughts about forsaking show business for a career teaching school or coaching sports in an inner city, but this idea never became reality. So in 1969, he did the closest thing by playing a coach on television. Cosby felt then, as he does now, that positive African-American role models are important on television. He said in 1968:

> It is the responsibility of TV and films to build a better image for the Negro. I see no reason why there can't be films with Negro cowboys who can shoot and ride and do all the things that people respect in a cowboy. Why can't there be black pilots in war stories?[13]

Chet Kincaid was to be that kind of role model. As the main character in Cosby's first situation comedy (simply titled *The Bill Cosby Show*), Chet was a gym teacher and coach in a moderately poor Los Angeles neighborhood. Kincaid was an intelligent teacher and a friend and advisor to his students. But Kincaid was also a human being, a man who was less than perfect and could learn a little himself now and then.

In one episode Kincaid scolds a student on the school football team who is a poor loser and feels winning is everything. He tells the student it is important to be a gracious loser.

Yet in the same episode, Kincaid complains and uses unsportsmanlike tactics to win a handball tournament. He loses anyway to an opponent using the same tactics, and the student gets the right message after seeing his own teacher acting as he did.

The Bill Cosby Show was a warmhearted program. It was placed in a tough time slot, Sunday from 8:30 to 9:00 P.M. It ran against the second half of the legendary *The Ed Sullivan Show*, a program that had been on the air since 1948.

Sullivan's show was a variety program, in which he acted as host and presented a succession of wide-ranging acts—performing animals, musical groups, and comedians. *The Ed Sullivan Show* is best known today for giving rock music legends Elvis Presley and The Beatles major exposure on television.

While Sullivan's ratings were not as high as they had been in earlier years, it was still formidable competition for Cosby. At first, *The Bill Cosby Show*'s ratings were quite good. It finished eleventh overall for the 1969–1970 season, was the highest rated new show, and easily beat Sullivan.[14]

The ratings for the second year fell sharply, and *The Bill Cosby Show* was cancelled after only two seasons.

Cosby took some heated criticism during the show's airing. And the criticisms were not necessarily related to the acting or writing. Some black activists condemned Cosby for not showing more inner city problems. They said that Chet Kincaid was a white man with black skin. These people missed the point, however, since Cosby was presenting a black man as a professional, a role model, and most importantly, a human being. Cosby felt that he was getting away from the negative stereotypes of blacks that so many whites had. Cosby would hear the same criticisms in later years as well.

By the time *The Bill Cosby Show* aired, the star and his wife had three children. A son, Ennis William Cosby, was born in April 1969.

Cosby soon decided that a change was necessary in his life.

6

Back to School and on to the Movies

Nearly ten years after dropping out of Temple University, Bill Cosby went back to college. But Cosby was not satisfied just to finish his bachelor's degree. His plans were to get a doctorate, the most advanced degree issued by any university.

Cosby decided to continue his education at the University of Massachusetts (UMass), located in the small town of Amherst in the western part of the state. After performing one time on the UMass campus in the late 1960s, Cosby told Dwight Allen, the university's dean of education, about his dream of going back to school. Allen urged Cosby to act on his dream.

Although Cosby lacked a bachelor's degree, UMass admitted him into their graduate program. The university concluded that what Cosby had learned

Bill Cosby decided to continue his education at the University of Massachusetts in Amherst. Shown here is a view of the campus.

through "lifetime experiences"—that is, the knowledge he acquired through his work—was equivalent to a bachelor's degree.

Allen said shortly after Cosby's acceptance, "We found by way of extensive testing that he's [Cosby's] sufficiently self-educated to meet our standards for admission to our graduate program. . . ."[1]

In time, Temple University would grant Cosby his bachelor's degree. The university decided he had earned it through the courses he was taking at UMass as well as lifetime experiences.

To be near school, Cosby and his family moved to a village near Amherst to live in a renovated farmhouse built in the 1850s. He officially entered the University of Massachusetts in 1971, and by August 1972, he earned a master's degree. This advanced degree was separate from his bachelor's and the next step toward earning his doctorate.

According to university rules, Cosby was free to come and go as he pleased as long as he did the required work. That was important since the combination entertainer and new student was embarking on two new television projects—both produced especially for children. And to work on these programs it was important that Cosby be free to travel to New York and Los Angeles.

With his interest in education, Cosby set out on a mission to design quality television programming for youngsters. The shows would be educational but entertaining. He did not want to lecture children or bore them with sermons.

He used some of the same material that appealed to adults, and created a cartoon television show featuring his childhood friends—Fat Albert, Weird Harold, and Dumb Donald. Each episode had a lesson for youngsters, but the shows were written so that kids would laugh while they learned. Called *Fat Albert and the Cosby Kids*, the cartoon program was aired on CBS on Saturday mornings and premiered on September 9, 1972.

Saturday morning has traditionally been devoted to children's shows. At the time that *Fat Albert and the Cosby Kids* went on the air, most other programs for kids were mindless cartoons with little value. In contrast, at the conclusion of every cartoon story, Fat Albert and the gang always learned something about growing up, accepting responsibility, or dealing with feelings such as anger or jealousy. At the end of each show, Cosby appeared to say a few words to his audience.

In one episode Dumb Donald's mother gives birth to a baby girl. Donald, until then an only child, has trouble accepting his new sister. Suddenly Donald cannot claim all his parents' attention and he has difficulty adjusting to that. But in time he learns to accept and even be proud of the new member of his family.

In the midst of studying for his doctorate degree, Bill Cosby also took time out to star in several special programs for television.

Then Cosby appears and advises the young people who have just finished watching the cartoon, "Parents are the best people to talk to if you have a problem like Donald's."[2]

In another show, a boy named Edward tells the gang that he spent the entire winter in Florida and came back as a champion swimmer. Edward was lying. He had never been to Florida and he could not even swim a lap in a duck pond. But the other boys have no reason not to believe him. So when summer comes around they make Edward show off his champion swimming techniques. Instead of admitting that he was lying, Edward tries to swim and nearly drowns, learning a lesson about lying and bragging.

During this time, Cosby commuted from Massachusetts to New York City to appear as a regular performer on *The Electric Company*. The purpose of this daily program on PBS (Public Broadcasting System) was to help children, ages seven to ten, build better reading skills. Cosby also sang and spoke on *The Electric Company* soundtrack album. In 1972 the album won a Grammy Award for best recording for children.

In 1971 Cosby showed a considerable amount of courage when he did a television special and recorded an album telling children about the problems caused by drug use. By the mid-1980s drug use had gotten so out of hand that it became fashionable for celebrities— including rock musicians, actors, and actresses—to do anti-drug commercials or give anti-drug talks at schools.

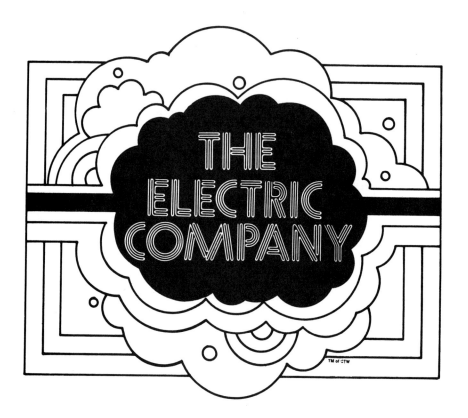

Bill Cosby appeared as a regular performer on *The Electric Company*, a daily program on PBS. *The Electric Company* name and logo are trademarks of the Children's Television Workshop.

But in 1971 drug use among young people and musicians was the fashion. The Vietnam War was still raging and seemed endless. In response, many young people resorted to drugs as an escape or a protest against the war and the establishment (the powerful people in government and major corporations seen as impersonal and greedy). For anyone in the entertainment business who related to young adults, speaking against drugs was risky, for it could make them seem part of the establishment.

Cosby was ahead of his time and foresaw the dangers of widespread drug use. On March 27, 1971, his television special *Bill Cosby Talks with Children about Drugs* was broadcast. He spoke with children about the dangers of drugs and the difficulty in recovering from addiction.

On the anti-drug record album *Bill Cosby Talks to Kids about Drugs*, Cosby discussed the advantages of a drug-free lifestyle. He said:

> The time spent acquiring a drug habit and kicking it is time you could have used to educate yourself. With an education you can become a valuable individual in your family, community, and nation. A junkie never caused freedom for any people.[3]

Since Cosby related to children and spoke to them, not down to them, neither his image nor his career suffered.

Cosby's audience was certainly getting an education, but in doing his research for his programs, Cosby was learning as well. So it was natural that he would combine his on-the-job learning with his pursuit for a doctoral degree.

Part of the requirement for earning a doctorate degree is a large report called a thesis. In a thesis the student promotes an original point of view based on research he or she has done. Cosby called his thesis, "An Integration of the Visual Media via *Fat Albert and the Cosby Kids* into the Elementary School Curriculum as a Teaching Aid and Vehicle to Achieve Increased Learning."

In more basic language, Cosby was discussing his own program and how it could be used to increase the quality of young children's education. He took advantage of his specialized studies to also help teachers, creating teacher's guides and workbooks that showed how to use the *Fat Albert and the Cosby Kids* cartoons in the classroom.

At the same time he was working on his studies and producing or performing in educational shows, Cosby continued to perform in nightclubs and to make records. Some were comedy records, others were musical; but not all were for children.

One record definitely was not for children. Cosby titled it *For Adults Only*, and it consisted of jokes about the intimate aspects of marriage and sex. It was a departure from his earlier albums, in which he talked about life as a child, and was a way of showing he could be funny about more than one subject.

He also released two music albums in the early 1970s. Both were called *Bill Cosby Presents Badfoot Brown and the Bunions Bradford Funeral and Marching Band*. However, there was no such marching band. The music was written and performed by Cosby and a few other musicians. In 1974 Cosby came out with another musical album called *At Last Bill Cosby Really Sings*. Success for the musical albums was modest.

Cosby even tried another nighttime television show. Just two days after *Fat Albert and the Cosby Kids* premiered on a Saturday morning, Cosby's new nighttime show debuted. Called *The New Bill Cosby Show*, it ran on CBS. This time Cosby did not play a character. The program was a variety show, and Cosby appeared as himself. He told jokes and acted in sketches with famous guest stars or regular co-stars.

The New Bill Cosby Show was put in the 10:00 P.M. time slot on Monday night, which proved to be a disaster. Young people who loved his humor had gone to bed long before the show went on the air. The show also followed two weak situation comedies at 9:00 and 9:30 P.M., so Cosby lacked a solid lead-in audience. Opposite him was the popular *Monday Night Football* on ABC. Furthermore variety shows were no longer successful the way they had been in the 1950s and 1960s. *The New Bill Cosby Show* had poor ratings and lasted only one year.

The cancellation of his show did not stop Cosby from keeping busy. He was about to enter a medium

Bill Cosby performing on *The New Bill Cosby Show*. Here Cosby is seen with actor William Wintersole.

that was completely new for him. While at least moderately successful with his live performances, record albums, and earlier television programs, Cosby had never before tackled the movies.

He had been offered movie roles similar to that of Alexander Scott, his character on *I Spy*. But Cosby wanted to try something different, something with more depth.

In response to his own question in 1968 about why there were no films about African-American cowboy heroes, he decided to take the matter into his own hands. He was shown a screenplay titled *Man and Boy*. The screenplay was about an African-American pioneer family trying to get by in the Old West in the years after the Civil War.

Cosby decided to make the screenplay into a movie. Cosby would play the hero, a man named Caleb Rever. Caleb loved his family and tried to make an honest living by working hard and living a dignified life in a time of prejudice and lawlessness.

Caleb wanted to establish a home for his wife and twelve-year-old son. One day, while in a mischievous mood, the son rode the family horse without his parents' permission, only to have it stolen. For a family starting out in that place and time, their horse was a most valuable possession. So the father and son travel together to find the horse. On their long journey they confront thugs, bigots, poor weather, and other forms of adversity.

The trouble was that no major studio wanted to take a chance on *Man and Boy*. Without any studio willing to produce the movie, it would be impossible to get the necessary money to pay the actors, camera crew, set designers, and all the other people necessary to make it successful.

It was 1971 and wholesome movies such as *Man and Boy* did not have the sex or violence audiences seemed to want at the time. Just two years earlier, an X-rated movie, *Midnight Cowboy*, won the Academy Award as best picture of the year. (*Midnight Cowboy* has since been reclassified with an R rating.)

The studio executives had other concerns too. Westerns seemed to be out of fashion on both television and in the movies. And many people were unaware of the roles African Americans had played in the settling of the West. One executive said the story was pure fiction, that there had been no African-American gunfighters in the Old West. He later read historic accounts and apologized. Cosby said, "They just didn't want to see that many black people in a cowboy picture."[4]

So Cosby decided to take on the major task of making *Man and Boy* himself. He found a partner and shot the movie on a skimpy budget of $800,000. This amount was incredibly low, considering that most movie productions at that time averaged $6 or $7 million.

When it was released in 1972, *Man and Boy* played in some theaters but not nearly as many as it would have if a major studio had produced it. It did not draw a lot of viewers into theaters, but because the initial investment was relatively small, it did not lose money.

The reviews were mixed. *The New York Times* gave the movie a thumbs down, but praised Cosby with: "As the star and engineer of an admirably economic project, *Man and Boy*, which genuinely tries to say something worthwhile, Bill Cosby is to be commended." The review indicated that with sharper dialogue and direction, "the film might have scored a neat home run. But at least it puts Mr. Cosby on first base in screen drama."[5]

With one movie under his belt, Cosby was ready to try again. This time he teamed up with his former buddy and co-star Robert Culp. The two again played men in law enforcement. In this movie, *Hickey and Boggs*, the pair were bumbling detectives—not intelligent under-cover spies. The reviews were again mixed, and financially, the movie was a failure.

The next movie to feature Cosby, *Uptown Saturday Night*, was both a financial and critical success. Released in 1974, it was directed by Sidney Poitier, a distinguished African-American actor. Poitier was tired of what seemed to be a steady stream of clichéd movies featuring African-American actors exclusively as sex-crazed detectives or sleazy criminals. Like Cosby had tried to achieve with *Man and Boy*, Poitier wanted a family movie with a predominantly African-American cast.

Uptown Saturday Night was a comedy set in the mostly black Harlem section of New York City. The story consisted of two friends, played by Cosby and Poitier, unwillingly involved with professional gangsters while searching for a missing lottery ticket.

Cosby, while never to become a movie superstar, proved in this film that he could capture an audience. He either starred or co-starred in one movie per year over the next four years.

All this time, Cosby was working on his doctoral degree and enlarging his family. Camille and Bill Cosby's fourth child, a girl named Ensa Camille, was born in 1973. And their fifth child, a girl named Evin Harrah, came into the world in 1975.

7

A Down Time

While on one hand Cosby's career and personal life seemed to be full of success, some dark clouds tarnished Cosby's image in the 1970s. Cosby started cultivating a difficult reputation in the early 1970s when reporters wrote that they found him impatient and arrogant.

Cosby has always valued his privacy and that of his family. His home in Massachusetts is off-limits to reporters and everyone but the family's closest friends. He has made it known that he gets tired of reporters misquoting him or asking personal questions.

He has said, "I hate it when writers try to psychoanalyze my life. I mean, how many of them have degrees in psychiatry?"[1]

In 1974, just before *Uptown Saturday Night* was released, Cosby did some radio advertisements in New

York City to promote the movie. One ad got him into trouble, branding him racially insensitive. Those who objected were not white, but black. Some blacks accused Cosby of stereotyping African Americans as criminals and low-lifes. In the ad Cosby said:

> Hi, this is Bill Cosby. Remember the good old days when you used to go uptown to Harlem and have a good time before it became very dangerous. Well, you can still go uptown without gettin' your head beat in by going downtown to see *Uptown Saturday Night*. This way the people are all on the screen and won't jump off and clean your head out. Bill Cosby, Sidney Poitier, Harry Belafonte, starring in *Uptown Saturday Night*. This is PG, parental guidance. I thank you.[2]

The ad ran for four days in early July on radio stations appealing to both white and African-American audiences. Negative reaction was swift. Residents of Harlem took the ad as a personal insult. Local African-American leaders blasted it. Walter Brecher, owner of the chain of theaters that included Harlem's Apollo Theater, called the ad "a vile characterization of a community" and "a dreadful slander." Brecher claimed that the ad was a marketing ploy, saying that if a movie opened in Harlem it would be labeled a black movie and white people would not want to see it.[3]

Cosby was in Europe when the incident took place, but he responded quickly, apologizing in a telegram:

> I wrote the blurb with the intent that it be humorous. Like lots of things humorous, sometimes a person has a lapse of taste. I retract it. I take back everything said and am sorry for any harm done. I apologize to the Harlem community and to black communities in all other cities. Had I listened to it after having done it, I'm certain I would have wiped it out myself.[4]

Cosby, who had always tried to promote the image of African Americans, learned a quick lesson about how even he could fall into a trap of insensitivity. By quickly apologizing, however, he showed both his maturity and respect for the African-American community.

The next year, 1975, Cosby starred in another film with Sidney Poitier titled *Let's Do It Again*. Money taken in at the New York premiere of the movie was donated to the YMCA and YWCA in Harlem.

A high point of Cosby's life was reached in May 1976. At the University of Massachusetts graduation ceremonies, Bill Cosby was awarded his doctor of education degree. He was now legally Dr. William H. Cosby, Jr.

Nearing the end of his studies at UMass, Cosby decided to make a commitment to another television show. This would also be a variety program similar to the one he did in the 1972–1973 season. But this program would air on ABC on Sunday at 7:00 P.M.—a

With his graduation from the University of Massachusetts in Amherst, Bill Cosby legally became Dr. William H. Cosby, Jr.

time when the kids who knew him from *The Electric Company* and *Fat Albert and the Cosby Kids* would still be awake.

At that time there were numerous television shows tackling controversial issues. The classic, ground-breaking situation comedy *All in the Family* is regarded as the first to frankly discuss subjects such as sexual matters and racism. In many ways *All in the Family* shocked people by focusing on these issues. But shock value aside, audiences found the show appealing, and it was the most watched television series for five seasons, from 1971 through 1976.

There is an old saying: "Nothing succeeds like success." So it was only natural that more comedies with dialogue and plots that dealt with sex and race hit the airwaves. Accepting the premise that there were few programs that all members of a family could watch together, the networks designated the prime time television hour from 8:00 to 9:00 P.M. (and 7:00 to 9:00 P.M. on Sunday) as the family hour.

Cosby agreed with that philosophy and his new program, *Cos*, was to be the perfect example of a family show. Unfortunately, it turned out to be a complete failure—lasting a mere seven weeks. The early hour in which the ABC network scheduled *Cos*, might have been ideal for children's schedules, but it also meant tough competition. On NBC was *The Wonderful World of Disney*, one of the few well-respected family shows

Bill Cosby has always been close to his mother, Anna. When Cosby dropped out of college, Mrs. Cosby thought he would never return. After receiving his doctorate from the University of Massachusetts, Cosby proved his proud mother wrong.

already running on television. And on CBS was the highly-rated television news magazine *60 Minutes.*

Most of the reviews of *Cos* were negative, however, indicating that the show might have been hindered by more than its time slot. Still, perhaps it was not the right time for a warm family show. President Richard Nixon had resigned his office in disgrace just two years earlier following the Watergate scandal. The lengthy Vietnam War had finally ended the previous year. After all the injured and lost lives and all the tumult caused by U.S. involvement, the plain fact was that the United States lost the war.

Americans were filled with cynicism and seemed to want to watch programs that sneered at authority and included dialogue with coarse language. One mid-1970s sitcom with a mostly African-American cast, *Baby I'm Back*, featured an Army colonel as a regular character and portrayed him as a buffoon.

Maybe Cosby was just in the wrong place at the wrong time. To the press, Cosby was matter-of-fact and humble about the failure, blaming only himself—not the time slot or the times he was living in. Cosby conceded:

> I have no animosity about TV, especially the fellows at ABC, because we did what we felt the people would want to see. But it's a very difficult area if you don't find the basic key. I don't think I can handle a weekly variety show. It has nothing to do with being too big for the medium or with race or anything else. I just haven't been able to put together the kind of show where the public will say, "Hey, let's watch!" It's as simple as that.[5]

His only real success at the time seemed to be as an actor in television commercials. He projected an image of trustworthiness, and so product manufacturers hired Cosby to be their spokesperson. Cosby was seen all hours of the day on television, doing commercials for products such as chocolate pudding and commercial airlines.

But his critics still attacked him from all sides. A writer from the *Village Voice*, an alternative newspaper in New York City, verbally clobbered Cosby with these words. "Cosby has become unfunny in recent years, a monotonous young fogey capitalizing wherever he can on his splendiferous teacher thing. . . . He has evolved into a kind of self-parodying sap."[6]

Cosby also fell out of favor with an unlikely group. The man who was a force in integrating television and who embodied a world of black and white cooperation was attacked by the Black Writers' Caucus, who did not seem to care what he had done in the past. The group publicly criticized him for having only two African-American staff writers on his show.

Even Cosby's humor was out of style. Audiences, both black and white, seemed to want to hear black comedians such as Richard Pryor. Pryor spoke in street dialect and swore frequently in his routines that relied heavily on racial humor.

Cosby made headlines for something less than complimentary in 1976. Perhaps as a reaction to all the negative press coverage, Cosby felt he had to let off some steam. Maybe he had reached his breaking point with the critics that seemed to be ganging up on him.

Comedian Tommy Smothers, who with his brother Dickie formed a popular comedy team called "The Smothers Brothers," approached Cosby at a party. Tommy Smothers and Cosby had never been the best of friends. Smothers had often criticized Cosby for not being a stronger voice in the civil rights movement. On this occasion, Smothers said he simply congratulated Cosby on his show *Cos*, not realizing it had just been cancelled.[7]

Cosby took it as a personal slight and wheeled around and punched Smothers in the face. Smothers fell to the floor like a piece of timber in the forest.

Cosby was known by his friends and co-workers as a man who easily angered. *I Spy* co-star Robert Culp once recalled that upon meeting Cosby in 1964, he felt he was the "angriest young man I'd ever met."[8]

Still, the public was shocked. Was this the Bill Cosby who they grew up with, who told all the funny stories about growing up, and who recalled the warmth of childhood and the human condition in his words?

Although it was a down time, Cosby still had his loyal following. He continued to make records, though sales had slowed. He was still a popular guest on the television program where he got his first national exposure, *The Tonight Show*. He filled the casino halls in Las Vegas. And he was still offered movie roles. But Cosby no longer seemed to have the magic touch he had earlier. Among certain segments of the public, it was fashionable to deride him.

Even his role in a popular 1978 movie *California Suite*, in which he co-starred with Richard Pryor, brought out criticism that seemed only he, or those he dragged along with him, could attract. The script for *California Suite* was written by award-winning playwright Neil Simon. It consisted of four separate sketches centering around guests at a posh hotel in Beverly Hills, California.

Cosby and Pryor played two doctors on vacation with their wives. Their roles were filled with physical slapstick comedy—furniture was smashed and the actors fell down or hit each other. The humor was similar to that in old Three Stooges or Laurel and Hardy films.

Pauline Kael, a movie critic from a widely-read magazine *The New Yorker*, accused the Cosby-Pryor sequences in the movie of being anti-black and the actors of mocking African Americans with their slapstick routines. She wrote:

> . . . the skit seems to be saying that the men may be doctors but they're still uncontrollable, dumb blacks who don't belong in a rich, civilized atmosphere . . . it all has horrifying racist overtones.[9]

It seemed that Cosby could not do anything right. To Cosby, Kael's criticism was worse than simply not liking his acting. Her intentions might have been noble, but Cosby felt her words smelled of hypocrisy. Kael is white, and Cosby resented a white person telling black people how they should act and what they could do.[10]

For decades, African Americans were limited to movie roles in which they played domestic workers or fools. Thanks to Cosby's work in *I Spy* and that of other African-American actors such as Sidney Poitier in honorable roles, African Americans were now accepted as intelligent, thinking human beings on stage, screen, and television. In *California Suite*, Cosby and Pryor were showing that the time had come when African-American actors could play any type of role—whether it be dignified or ridiculous.

Cosby was so upset that he placed an advertisement in *Variety*, a trade publication for the entertainment business. He asked why black actors should be treated with different standards than white actors. He later explained:

> I became enraged when I read that because her own racism would not allow her to see two guys who were taking the same liberties—tearing up a hotel room—as Laurel and Hardy and the Marx Brothers were permitted to take. . . . Suppose, as a kid, I wanted to grow up and be like Charlie Chaplin. That doesn't mean I want to grow up to be white. It means I want to be funny, to bump into a pole, to fall in love with a beautiful woman and be very clumsy about giving her a rose.[11]

This incident seemed typical of Bill Cosby's life in the late 1970s.

8

"Hard to Get Good Help, Isn't It?"

Bill Cosby began the 1980s in the same manner in which he had ended the 1970s. He was best known for his appearances on *The Tonight Show* and seemed to be all over people's television screens doing commercials. He often appeared live in Lake Tahoe and Las Vegas. In 1983 he made a movie of his comedy act called *Bill Cosby Himself.*

That same year he teamed up with an entertainment legend, singer and dancer Sammy Davis, Jr., to do a two-man show in Las Vegas. Called *Sammy and Cos,* the show was a smash. The two show business veterans decided to take *Sammy and Cos* to Broadway, with its more sophisticated and seasoned New York audiences. But there the show ended shortly after it had begun its run.

By the beginning of 1984, Cosby had acquired the image of a career funnyman, a comedian who could always be counted on to make an audience laugh with an amusing tale about his home life or to sell a product with a smile on television. He was still earning money and drawing crowds, but it seemed as if his glory days were long gone. He had not achieved any real innovative success in over a decade. His career had leveled off since the rave reviews of the 1960s and early 1970s.

One night around midnight in the early 1980s, Cosby decided to watch some cable television while his wife and children were sleeping. Even though he became a star on television, Cosby tried to limit watching television in his home. He preferred that his children read books and converse instead. That night he was in for an awakening. He recalled:

> I saw three movies about rape. They all seemed designed to do the same thing—show women having their clothes torn off, show the violence of a man taking a woman, show a woman screaming for help.

> The next night I watched again. This time I heard people cursing for no reason other than to get a laugh. Once more, the woman was never shown doing anything practical, never demonstrating she could get along in life without a man.[1]

Cosby also said, "My kids, if unmonitored, could watch four different movies showing cars smashing, people getting drunk, and sex without permission as entertainment."[2]

After discussing with his wife what he had witnessed on television, Cosby had the urge to do a television series that parents could watch with their children.

Cosby considered doing a detective show, since the format was popular then. But instead of solving matters with guns, he would solve them with his brains. His partner would be a woman who was strong, intelligent, and had her own career.

The idea was turned down by the three major networks—NBC, CBS, and ABC—since they thought the airwaves were saturated with detective shows.

So he tried another idea, a situation comedy about a strong African-American family with lots of humor and love, but with no blatant sex or violence. He pitched it to network executives. Like his idea about the detective show, reactions were negative.

Some executives said that the latest marketing studies indicated that the concept of the situation comedy was dead.[3] In the television season of 1983–1984, eight of the top-ten prime time shows were either soap operas filled with sex or detective shows loaded with violence. The only exceptions were the long-running news magazine *60 Minutes*, and one comedy called *Kate & Allie*, a low-key show about two single women sharing a house and raising children. With only one situation comedy in the year's top ten, it seemed to many executives that widely watched sitcoms were a trend of the past.

But Cosby did not give up. He interested a production company called Carsey-Werner in the idea and made a pilot about Heathcliff (Cliff) Huxtable, a doctor married to Claire Huxtable, a woman lawyer. Together, the couple raises four children from grade school to high school age. Perhaps in order to spice up the show and interest executives who were down on the idea of a wholesome program in 1984, Cosby wrote a sketch for the pilot in which the father talked to his daughters about sex.

"That's what sold the show," reported Cosby. He added that NBC Entertainment President Brandon Tartikoff "obviously felt that there was enough amusing and educational material in the stories about my wife and children that I had been using for years in my nightclub act."[4]

So NBC took a chance on *The Cosby Show* in the same way that they had taken a chance on *I Spy* almost twenty years earlier. The program was first telecast on September 20, 1984.

Who could have expected *The Cosby Show* to be the success it was? At the end of its first season it ranked as the third most watched prime time television show for the season. For the next five seasons *The Cosby Show* ranked number one each year. (After the show had aired a while, a fifth child, college-aged daughter Sondra, was

The original cast of *The Cosby Show*, starring Bill Cosby. The show ranked number one for five consecutive seasons.

added to the cast. Her earlier absence was explained by saying she had been away at college.)

The Cosby Show had been on the air just over a year when NBC Entertainment President Tartikoff said, "Bill Cosby is not just the biggest star in television. He's become the biggest star in America."[5]

Episodes focused on kinds of events that could happen in any family. In one classic episode, the youngest child, Rudy, is moved to tears because her pet goldfish dies. Cliff soothes her hurt feelings by holding a special funeral for the fish at the toilet bowl in the family bathroom.

At other times two sisters sharing a single room might argue over who is taking up more space, or teenaged son Theo might spend all his hard-earned money buying a fake ring to impress a girl who could not care less about him.

Heathcliff Huxtable was a bit of a curmudgeon; he loved his kids, but did not mind using a little sarcasm now and then. In one episode he walks into his son's room and nearly trips over all the junk on the floor.

"Hard to get good help, isn't it?" he says to Theo, as a not-so-subtle way of telling him to clean up his room.[6]

Like the female character Cosby had wanted to place in his detective show, Claire Huxtable was a strong and smart career woman. Cosby felt it was important that both Cliff and Claire were equal partners in their marriage, reflecting his own personal views.

> If I play tennis with a woman, I don't mind if she's a better player than I am. It doesn't make my life miserable if I lose to a woman. I don't mind seeing an integrated [male and female] basketball game. And certainly, I don't mind male elementary school teachers when everybody thinks that job is a woman's role.[7]

Insisting that his show be both realistic and educational, Cosby hired a production consultant. His name was Dr. Alvin F. Poussaint and he was a professor of psychiatry at Harvard Medical School in Cambridge, Massachusetts. Cosby had worked with Dr. Poussaint on documentaries in the 1970s.

Poussaint explained, "Cosby wanted me to make sure we showed people respect and that no characters were treated in a stereotypical manner."[8]

It was up to Poussaint to suggest changes for any lines or actions he found objectionable. One change he made was on a Halloween episode. The script called for one of the children to dress like Captain Hook, the villain from *Peter Pan*, who had a hook instead of a hand. Poussaint noted that the idea of disabled people portrayed as villains was an unfair stereotype. The costume was changed.

Another episode called for Claire to be combing Rudy's hair when Rudy says, "Ouch, you're hurting

Dr. Alvin F. Poussaint worked as a production consultant on *The Cosby Show.*

me." Poussaint suggested that as she combs Rudy's hair, Claire tells Rudy that her hair is beautiful, so viewers would not believe the idea that black people's hair is undesirable.

Poussaint continued, saying that Cosby also wanted his sitcom to be psychologically believable:

> He noticed other sitcoms had a lot of one-liners but no real story line. He wanted people to look at each show and say, "That really happened in our house.' He wanted to send an educational message.
>
> Cosby felt too many sitcoms were using insult humor and put-downs, making fun of people because they were fat or skinny or because of the clothes they wore. He wanted to get away from that.[9]

Unlike other predominantly black programs, *The Cosby Show* plots did not revolve around race. Poussaint said, "Cosby felt that too many black shows were preoccupied with race issues. He was taking a positive tack, showing a black family that could love each other without race always intruding."[10]

Time magazine commended *The Cosby Show* for being "the first all-black sitcom to eschew jivey jargon and negative stereotypes."[11]

But it was clear that the Huxtables were proud of their African-American heritage. Poussaint noted that one of his roles was to make sure that the Huxtables did not ignore their heritage.

Malcolm Jamal Warner played the character of Theo on *The Cosby Show*. He is shown here with TV dad Bill Cosby.

"If one of the children had to do a book report and the script had her doing a book by Norman Mailer (a white author), I would suggest *Invisible Man* by Ralph Ellison (a black author) instead," Poussaint said.[12]

In addition, the Huxtables had works by black artists hanging on their living room wall. And when the oldest daughter gave birth to twins, she and her husband named them Winnie and Nelson, in honor of the South African human rights activists, Winnie and Nelson Mandela.

At one point, son Theo posted a sign reading "Abolish Apartheid" on his bedroom wall. (Apartheid was the name for the policy of legalized segregation in South Africa in effect at the time.) The sign in itself caused controversy. Network censors wanted it removed, saying that the network could not be seen supporting any issue in which there are two sides. Cosby responded angrily:

> There may be two sides to apartheid in Archie Bunker's house [Archie Bunker was the bigoted lead character on *All in the Family*]. But it is impossible that the Huxtables would be on any side but one. That sign will stay on the door. And I've told NBC that if they still want it down, or if they try to edit it out, there will be no show.[13]

The sign stayed. Today it is not uncommon for other television programs, such as *Murphy Brown*, to show signs or bumper stickers in the background representing their characters' views.

Bill Cosby with Raven Symone, who played Cosby's granddaughter
Olivia on the top-rated show.

Cosby also displayed his interest in formal education on the program by often wearing sweatshirts bearing the names of predominantly black colleges. Many people tried to guess from one week to the next which college's sweatshirt Cosby would be wearing on the next week's show.

The show had its critics, as any show does—no matter how popular. Some said that the Huxtables were an unrealistic portrayal of a black family in America and that the show would cause white people to become unconcerned about the many blacks living in poverty. Critics said that the positive family situation on *The Cosby Show* might even cause white people to think that all blacks' problems had been solved.

These critics missed the point of the show, which was explained by Cosby:

> To say the Huxtables are not black enough is a denial of the American dream and the American way of life. My point is that this is an American family—an *American* family—and if you want to live like they do, and if you're willing to work, the opportunity is there.[14]

Cosby's former collaborator and co-star Sidney Poitier responded, "One of the unfortunate things about television is that the black middle class is never seen. We see an awful lot of guys pushing dope on street corners."[15]

Erika Alexander, who portrayed cousin Pam on *The Cosby Show*, represented a character from a low income background. She is seen here with Bill Cosby.

Coretta Scott King, the civil rights activist and widow of Dr. Martin Luther King, Jr., also defended *The Cosby Show*. She said:

> The show is certainly the most positive portrayal of black family life that has ever been broadcast. With one out of every three black families living below the poverty line, it is inspiring to see a black family that has managed to escape the violence of poverty through education and unity.[16]

Dr. Alvin Poussaint responded:

> One program can't show all aspects of the black experience any more than one can show all aspects of the white community. But we did deal with issues like crime, teenage pregnancy, drugs, and AIDS, especially in the last couple of seasons when the role of Pam, a cousin from a low income background who came to live with the family, was written into the show.[17]

The Cosby Show even spawned a successful spin-off. (A spin-off is a completely new television program based on a character from an existing one.) In 1987 the Huxtables' second oldest daughter, Denise, played by Lisa Bonet, left home after graduating high school to attend predominantly black Hillman College. Denise was following a family tradition, since both Heathcliff and his father had also attended Hillman.

The new show about Denise's college adventures was a situation comedy called *A Different World*. Bonet left *A Different World* after one season, but the show continued to run for several years with other characters.

There are many reasons why some television shows become hits while others fail. Certainly much has to do with the writing, the chemistry among the actors, and the quality of the performances.

Another reason is timing. The mood of the United States in 1984 was much different than that in 1976. After what seemed like two decades of disasters, including the Vietnam War, the Watergate scandal, and the Iranian hostage crisis, Americans wanted to feel good about themselves. The American people had an optimistic attitude about their life and their country. The economy was strong and in spite of actual social trends, traditional values were on Americans' minds. The time had come for a television program such as *The Cosby Show*. Poussaint offered his explanation:

> *The Cosby Show* came on the air when the traditional family was beginning to be disrupted with dual career couples, and the show was extremely positive in a way families felt things ought to be. Here was a two-career couple, both professionals, who were role models. They negotiated with their kids, rather than just shouting at them. Most parents on television at the time were portrayed as kind of weak. The Huxtables were strong and firm, but the family was very democratic.[18]

Even in its last year on the air, *The Cosby Show* rated in the top ten. The expanded cast of the show is shown here.

But there was perhaps one more reason. That had to do with Bill Cosby and his humorous way of dealing with life's problems. His humor was gentle and understated. And the Huxtable kids did not say precocious or overly cute things that children would never say in real life. The show was real, and people liked that about it.

The Cosby Show ran for eight seasons and was a top-ten show even in its last year. By then the nation's economy had soured and the mood of the country had reverted to one of cynicism. The last episode of *The Cosby Show* aired on April 30, 1992.

9

A Man of Talent and Generosity

While *The Cosby Show* gave a jump start to Bill Cosby's career, it also launched him into another field of endeavor: writing. Cosby had written two books in the 1970s: *Fat Albert's Survival Guide* for children, and *Bill Cosby's Personal Guide to Tennis Power*, a humorous look at tennis instruction.

When, in 1986, Cosby decided to capitalize on his role as Heathcliff Huxtable, America's favorite father, his writing career really exploded. Cosby released *Fatherhood*, a collection of witty, warm, and somewhat sarcastic essays about bringing up children. The following selection is typical:

> Unless he happens to work for Halston, the American father cannot be trusted to put together combinations of clothes. He is a man who was

taught that the height of fashion was to wear two shoes that matched; and so, children can easily convince him of the elegance of whatever they do or don't want to wear.

"Dad, I don't want to wear socks today."

"Fine."

"Or a shirt."

"That's fine, too."

Mothers, however, are relentless in dressing children and often draw tears.

"Young lady, you are not going to wear red leotards outside this house unless you're on your way to dance *Romeo and Juliet.*"

"But, Mom, everyone at *school* is wearing them."

"Then I'm helping you keep your individuality. You're wearing that nice gray skirt with the blue sweater and the white lace blouse."

"But, Mom, I *hate* that white blouse. It makes me look like a *waitress.*"

"Which is what you'll be if you don't wear it 'cause you won't be leaving the house to go to school, and a restaurant job will be *it.*"[1]

Fatherhood set a modern-day record with a total of $2.6 million sales of the hardcover edition. The book was on the best-seller list for over a year.[2]

Buoyed by the success of *Fatherhood,* Cosby wrote a sequel called *Time Flies,* published in 1987. *Time Flies* was written in the same style as *Fatherhood,* although the topic changed from raising children to getting older. Cosby began *Time Flies* with:

> I recently turned fifty, which is young for a tree, mid-life for an elephant, and ancient for a quarter-miler, whose son now says, 'Dad, I just can't run the quarter with you unless I bring something to read.'[3]

Time Flies was another sensation. The first printing of most authors' books run in the range of 3,000 to 10,000. The first printing of *Time Flies* was an astounding record of 1.75 million copies.[4]

Cosby followed those two successes with two more books: *Love and Marriage* in 1989 and *Childhood* in 1991. Yet while he had remarkable success as a television actor and author, Cosby never reached the same level of superstardom in the movies. Two movies he made in the late 1980s—*Leonard, Part 6* and *Ghost Dad*, both comedies—received poor reviews and drew few people to theaters.

Cosby himself was critical of *Leonard, Part 6*. In November 1987, he appeared on *Larry King Live* on CNN and distanced himself from his movie. Cosby said:

> It is not my picture. I don't want them [his fans] to go see this movie thinking that I'm saying to them that this is a great picture, or that this is even a good picture. . . . It might be better that these people wait and have their friends tell them if they like it or not.[5]

In spite of his moderate success in movies, in the 1990s Cosby ranks as one of the wealthiest people in show business. Along with his Massachusetts home, Cosby has other homes in New York City, Philadelphia, Los Angeles, and Las Vegas. A well-respected business magazine, *Forbes*, publishes an annual list of top-earning entertainers. In recent years, Cosby has ranked either number one or close to it. Cosby laughed about the listing in 1991, saying:

> The only joke I ever get out of it comes when I go by the newsstand to pick up my papers. Sometimes I don't have enough change and I say to the guy, "I'll pay you when I come back the next time." When I dropped out of number one, the guy says, "No! You leave the paper here, then you come back. You're number three now." Since I'm back to number one, he says, "You don't have to pay me now."[6]

With the enormous wealth he has accumulated Cosby has also acquired power. In 1992 Cosby attempted to buy NBC. But even with all his money, Cosby could not afford to buy an entire network on his own. NBC is worth well into the billions of dollars. But with the assistance of some powerful investors, the purchase was possible. Cosby was told that NBC was not for sale at the time, but network executives became aware that Cosby could wield significant clout.[7]

However, power cannot dictate people's viewing habits. In September 1992, Cosby signed a contract to host *You Bet Your Life*. This television quiz show was to offer an outlet for Cosby's humor. The show had been a hit on NBC from 1950 to 1961 when legendary comedian and movie actor Groucho Marx hosted it. The program was more chitchat and comedy than questions and answers. Critics thought Cosby would have the same rapport with audiences that Marx had. The program would also be taped in Cosby's hometown of Philadelphia.

Cosby put his personal stamp on *You Bet Your Life*. Marx offered $100 to any contestant who said on the air the "secret word," a common word chosen prior to the contestant's appearance and without the contestant's knowledge. If someone said the "secret word" a fake stuffed duck was lowered from the ceiling. Cosby offered a prize of $500, and instead of a duck, he used a black goose wearing a Temple University sweatshirt.

A man named George Fenniman served as Marx's sidekick. Cosby selected a woman, Robbi Chong, as his partner. She is the daughter of Tommy Chong, a comedian popular in the 1960s and 1970s and half of a comedy team called Cheech and Chong. She was thrilled to work with Cosby, saying, "There's always such a nice, relaxed feeling when working with him that you just don't ever want to leave."[8]

Unlike Cosby's other television programs, which ran on networks, *You Bet Your Life* was syndicated. This meant that any one television station in any community, regardless of its network affiliation, could air the show.

But *You Bet Your Life* did not succeed and was off the air in a year.

In 1994 Cosby teamed up again with his old co-star and friend Robert Culp to do an *I Spy* sequel, catching up on the adventures of Robinson and Scott nearly thirty years later. Sheldon Leonard, now in his eighties, produced it. This time it was aired on CBS—not on NBC, where the original *I Spy* series was aired. Again, people watched. Leonard said:

> The ratings were very good considering the fact that they put it against the toughest competition, *Seinfeld*, on NBC. What they were using the sequel for was not so much to win a high rating for themselves but to diminish the rating for the opposition. It's a game they play and a game I hate and it's one of the reasons I am very reluctant to get re-involved in television.[9]

Cosby was not finished doing detective work on television yet. He starred in a two-hour mystery movie made for television, which was shown on NBC in early 1994. He played a retired criminologist named Guy Hanks. (The name of Cosby's character is a tribute to his wife, Camille. Hanks was her maiden name.)

Since the movie received good ratings, NBC decided to turn the movie's story line into a regular series. In September 1994, *The Cosby Mysteries*—with Cosby playing Guy Hanks—premiered on Wednesday evenings at 8:00 P.M.

The New York Times reported in a review that *The Cosby Mysteries* was "likely to appeal to older viewers eager to escape the escalating nastiness and violence of real life. The bad guys never get away with anything in this tightly structured world."[10]

The overall review was mixed, however. The *Times* said Cosby was charming, but the mystery plots were weak.[11]

The Cosby Mysteries did not catch on immediately with the public the way that *The Cosby Show* had ten years earlier. The ratings for the first several episodes were adequate, but not noteworthy. The program usually ranked between 40th and 45th place out of some 90 prime time weekly television shows. At the end of the first season, the network decided not to renew the series.

Regardless of wherever his latest projects might take him, Cosby has already made his mark in television history. In 1992 he received an honor given to a select number of lifetime achievers in television. He was inducted into the Television Arts and Sciences Hall of Fame. Appropriately, Sheldon Leonard was by his side, also being inducted at the same time, along with four others.

Cosby used the occasion to offer his thanks, but also to blast the depiction of African Americans on television, since *The Cosby Show* was no longer on the air. It seemed that all the television programs with mostly African-American stars portrayed the characters as jive-talking and wise-cracking kids. By trying to be hip, the networks had resorted back to stereotypes. Cosby said angrily:

None of these images happen to be the kind of people that you can imagine graduating from college, that you can imagine working beside in a steel mill and seriously thinking about their family, about their life, about their contribution to making a better United States and world.[12]

Interestingly, while he writes and jokes about family life, Cosby is still very private about his real family. Bill and Camille are still married and observers say they are still as much in love as ever. His co-star from his 1980s television show *The Cosby Show*, Phylicia Rashad, said, "I've seen Bill walk into a crowded room, suddenly spot her and start crawling toward her across the floor. Every time he looks at her, it's as if he's seeing her for the first time. It's like they're still on a high school date."[13]

When not at work Cosby relaxes on the tennis court or listens to jazz. He is a generous philanthropist, serving on the advisory boards of several foundations and charities such as the Black Film Foundation and the American Sickle Cell Foundation.

As one might expect, Cosby maintains a special interest in education. He is a member of the Communications Council of Howard University. (Howard is a predominantly black university in Washington, D.C.)

In 1993 he launched a campaign to promote racial harmony at his alma mater, the University of Massachusetts, by speaking at a conference on race relations. The university campus had been the site of racial incidents in recent years.

In September 1996, Cosby gave television another try. He stars in a situation comedy called simply *Cosby*.

In early 1997, Cosby was in the news for some unfortunate reasons. On January 16, his son, Ennis, was shot to death while changing a tire on a Los Angeles freeway. (In March, a suspect was arrested in Ennis's murder. The motive was allegedly robbery.)

Coincidentally, Cosby's friend Sheldon Leonard had died just five days before Ennis's murder. At the end of the January 20 episode of his television show, Cosby paid tribute to both his son and Leonard. Under Leonard's picture a caption read, "My last father." [14]

In an unrelated incident soon afterwards, a young woman sued Cosby. She claimed that Cosby was her natural father. Cosby admitted that he had a brief illicit affair with her mother some twenty years earlier.[15] However, he insisted he was not her father.[16] The woman and a male friend were arrested and charged with trying to extort $24 million from Cosby.[17]

In a rare public statement, Camille Cosby said, "All old personal negative issues between Bill and me were resolved years ago. We are a united couple."[18]

In his first stage appearance after Ennis's murder on February 1, 1997, Cosby told the audience, "I want you all to know, you don't have to forget what happened. But we're supposed to laugh, have a good time . . . God bless all of you, and thank you for your hearts."[19]

Chronology

1937—Born in Philadelphia, Pennsylvania, on July 12.

1956—Drops out of high school and enlists in U.S. Navy.

1960—Enrolls at Temple University in Philadelphia.

1962—Works at The Gaslight in Greenwich Village section of New York City; drops out of Temple.

1963—Has first appearance on network television on *The Tonight Show*; first album *Bill Cosby Is a Very Funny Fellow . . . Right!* is released.

1964—Marries Camille Hanks on January 25.

1965—Daughter Erika is born.

1965–1968—Stars in *I Spy*.

1966—Daughter Erinn is born.

1969—Son Ennis William is born.

1969–1971—Stars in *The New Bill Cosby Show*.

1971—Enrolls in graduate school at the University of Massachusetts.

1972—Earns master's degree from the University of Massachusetts; *Fat Albert and the Cosby Kids* first appears on television; stars in first movie, *Man and Boy*.

1972–1973—Stars in *The New Bill Cosby Show*.

1973—Daughter Ensa Camille is born.

1974—Appears in *Uptown Saturday Night*.

1975—Daughter Evin Harrah is born.

1976—Earns Doctorate of Education from University of Massachusetts; variety show *Cos* has brief run on network television.

1978—Appears in movie *California Suite.*

1983—Stars in movie version of his nightclub act titled *Bill Cosby Himself.*

1984—Stars in *The Cosby Show.*
-1992

1986—*Fatherhood* is published.

1987—*Time Flies* is published.

1988—Donates $20 million to Spelman College, largest donation ever by one person to a black college.

1989—*Love and Marriage* is published.

1991—*Childhood* is published.

1992—Announces interest in buying NBC; stars as host of *You Bet Your Life*; is inducted into Television Arts and Sciences Hall of Fame.

1994—Co-stars with Robert Culp in *I Spy* sequel; stars in *The Cosby Mysteries.*

Places to Visit

California

NBC Studios, 3000 West Almeda Avenue, Burbank—Hourly tours include special effects demonstrations, sound effects room, wardrobe, make-up department, and a studio. (818) 840-4444, extension 3537.

Illinois

Museum of Broadcast Communications, 78 East Washington Street, Chicago—Old televisions and radios are displayed, and a huge library offers TV videotapes for your viewing. You can also anchor your own "newscast." (312) 629-6000.

New York

Museum of Television and Radio, 25 West 52nd Street, Manhattan—Visitors can watch selected videotapes from a vast library. Special exhibits are often scheduled. (212) 621-6800 or (212) 621-6200.

Pennsylvania

Afro-American Historical and Cultural Museum, 7th and Arch Streets, Philadelphia—Achievements of African Americans in varied fields, such as business, music, politics, and entertainment are presented through exhibits, photographs, and multi-media presentations. (215) 574-0380.

Washington D.C.

National Museum of American History, of the Smithsonian Institution, Constitution Avenue—The museum contains a large gallery devoted to the impact of television on American history. (202) 357-2700.

Selected Discography

Spoken Word Albums

Bill Cosby Is a Very Funny Fellow . . . Right! (Warner Bros., 1963.)

I Started Out as a Child. (Warner Bros., 1964.)

Why Is There Air? (Warner Bros., 1965.)

Wonderfulness. (Warner Bros., 1966.)

Revenge. (Warner Bros., 1967.)

To Russell, My Brother Whom I Slept With. (Warner Bros., 1968.)

200 MPH. (Warner Bros., 1968.)

It's True, It's True. (Warner Bros., 1969.)

8:15 12:15. (Tetragrammaton, 1969.)

Bill Cosby: Sports. (UNI, 1969.)

Live at Madison Square Garden Center. (UNI, 1970.)

When I Was a Kid. (UNI, 1971.)

For Adults Only. (UNI, 1971.)

Inside the Mind of Bill Cosby. (UNI, 1972.)

Fat Albert. (MCA, 1973.)

My Father Confused Me, What Must I Do. (Capitol, 1977.)

Bill's Best Friend. (Capitol, 1978.)

Bill Cosby Himself. (Motown, 1982.)

Bill Cosby/Hardheaded Boys. (Nicetown, 1985.)

Those of You With or Without Children, You'll Understand. (Geffen, 1986.)

Oh Baby. (Geffen, 1991.)

Music Albums

Bill Cosby Sings/"Silver Throat." (Warner Bros., 1967.)

Hooray for the Salvation Army Band. (Warner Seven Arts, 1968.)

Bill Cosby Presents Badfoot Brown and the Bunions Bradford Funeral and Marching Band. (UNI, 1970.)

Bill Cosby Presents Badfoot Brown and the Bunions Bradford Funeral and Marching Band. (Sussex/Buddah, 1972.)

At Last Bill Cosby Really Sings. (Partee, 1974.)

Bill Cosby Is Not Himself These Days, Rat Own, Rat Own, Rat Own. (Capitol, 1976.)

Disco Bill. (Capitol, 1977.)

Compilation Albums

Best of Bill Cosby. (Warner Bros., 1969.)

More of the Best of Bill Cosby. (Warner Bros., 1970.)

Bill. (MCA, 1973.)

Other Albums

Diana: The Original TV Soundtrack. (Motown, 1971.)

The Congressional Black Caucus. (Black Forum, 1972.)

The Electric Company Soundtrack. (Warner Bros., 1972.)

Bill Cosby Talks to Kids About Drugs. (MCA, 1971.)

Chapter Notes

Chapter 1

1. Personal interview with Sheldon Leonard, March 15, 1994.

2. Ibid.

3. Ronald L. Smith, *Cosby* (New York: St. Martin's Press, 1986), p. 63.

4. "Color Him Funny," *Newsweek*, January 31, 1966, p. 76.

Chapter 2

1. Bill Adler, *The Cosby Wit: His Life and Humor* (New York: Carroll & Graf Publishers, 1986), p. 13.

2. Ronald L. Smith, *Cosby* (New York: St. Martin's Press, 1986), p. 2.

3. Ibid.

4. Ibid., p. 3.

5. Caroline Latham, *Bill Cosby—For Real* (New York: TOR Books, 1985), p. 11.

6. Ibid., p. 13.

7. Louie Robinson, "The Pleasures and Problems of Being Bill Cosby," *Ebony*, July 1969, p. 151.

8. Latham, p. 13.

9. Adler, p. 14.

10. Smith, p. 18.

11. Latham, p. 19.

12. Dan Goodgame and Bill Cosby, "I Do Believe in Control," *Time*, September 28, 1987, p. 64.

13. Adler, p. 15.

Chapter 3

1. Personal interview with Gavin White, March 15, 1994.

2. Ibid.

3. Ibid.

4. Ibid.

5. Ronald L. Smith, *Cosby* (New York: St. Martin's Press, 1986), p. 27.

6. Paul Gardner, "Comic Turns Quips Into Tuition," *The New York Times*, June 25, 1962, p. 23.

Chapter 4

1. Bob Thomas, "Cosby Talks," *Good Housekeeping*, February 1991, p. 214.

2. Bill Adler, *The Cosby Wit: His Life and Humor* (New York: Carroll and Graf Publishers, 1986), pp. 17–18.

3. Paul Gardner, "Comic Turns Quips Into Tuition," *The New York Times*, June 25, 1962, p. 23.

4. Personal interview with Gavin White, March 15, 1994.

5. Ibid.

6. Ibid.

7. Ronald L. Smith, *Cosby* (New York: St. Martin's Press, 1986), p. 47.

8. Caroline Latham, *Bill Cosby—For Real* (New York: TOR Books, 1989), p. 30.

9. Harold and Geraldine Woods, *Bill Cosby: Making America Laugh and Learn* (Minneapolis: Dillon Press, 1983), pp. 25–27.

10. Ibid., p. 27.

11. Muriel Davidson, "Celebrating With the Bill Cosbys," *Good Housekeeping*, December 1972, p. 144.

Chapter 5

1. Allan Sherman, *Hello Muddah, Hello Fadduh! (A Letter From Camp)*, Warner Records, 1963.

2. Bill Adler, *The Cosby Wit: His Life and Humor* (New York: Carroll & Graf Publishers, 1986), p. 20.

3. Allan Sherman, liner notes on record album *Bill Cosby Is a Very Funny Fellow . . . Right!*, 1963.

4. Ibid.

5. Personal interview with Sheldon Leonard, March 15, 1994.

6. Ibid.

7. Ibid.

8. Ibid.

9. Ibid.

10. Ibid.

11. Ibid.

12. Joel Whitburn, *The Billboard Book of Top 40 Hits*, 4th ed. (New York: Billboard Publications, 1989), p. 105.

13. Art Peters, "What the Negro Wants from TV," *TV Guide* article from 1968 reprinted in *TV Guide, The First 25 Years*, compiled and edited by Jay S. Harris (New York: Simon & Schuster, 1968), p. 142.

14. Tim Brooks and Earle Marsh, *The Complete Directory to Prime Time Network TV Shows, 1946–Present* (New York: Ballantine Books, 1992), p. 1100.

Chapter 6

1. Muriel Davidson, "Celebrating With the Bill Cosbys," *Good Housekeeping*, December 1972, p. 146.

2. Ann Feltmann, "Laughing and Learning with Bill Cosby," *Parents*, September 1974, p. 46.

3. Ibid., p. 48.

4. Louie Robinson, "Man and Boy," *Ebony*, April 1971, p. 43.

5. Howard Thompson, "Cosby in *Man and Boy*," *The New York Times*, March 16, 1972, p. 59.

Chapter 7

1. Harry F. Waters, "Cosby's Fast Track," *Newsweek*, September 2, 1985, p. 52.

2. Mel Gussow, "Movie Ad Called Slur on Harlem," *The New York Times*, July 11, 1974, p. 24.

3. Ibid.

4. "Cosby Apologizes for *Uptown* Ad," *The New York Times*, July 16, 1974, p. 41.

5. Louie Robinson, "Dr. Bill Cosby," *Ebony*, June 1977, p. 136.

6. Ronald L. Smith, *Cosby* (New York: St. Martin's Press, 1986), p. 151.

7. Ronald L. Smith, *The Cosby Book* (New York: S.P.I. Books, 1993), p. 202.

8. Don Goodgame and Bill Cosby, "I Do Believe in Control," *Time,* September 28, 1987, p. 59.

9. Pauline Kael, "Simon and Ross—The Compassion Boys," *The New Yorker*, January 8, 1979, p. 50.

10. Waters, p. 56.

11. Ibid.

Chapter 8

1. Bill Davidson, "I Must Be Doing Something Right," *McCall's*, April 1985, p. 147.

2. Todd Gold, "Bill Cosby: The Doctor Is In," *Saturday Evening Post*, April 1985, p. 42.

3. Ibid.

4. Davidson, p. 147.

5. Harry F. Waters, "Cosby's Fast Track," *Newsweek*, September 2, 1985, p. 52.

6. Harry F. Waters and Peter McAlevey, "Bill Cosby Comes Home," *Newsweek*, November 5, 1984, p. 93.

7. Bob Thomas, "Cosby Talks," *Good Housekeeping*, February 1991, p. 215.

8. Personal interview with Dr. Alvin Poussaint, April 12, 1994.

9. Ibid.

10. Ibid.

11. Waters and McAlevey, p. 93.

12. Personal interview with Dr. Alvin F. Poussaint, April 12, 1994.

13. Waters, p. 51.

14. Dan Goodgame and Bill Cosby, "I Do Believe in Control," *Time*, September 28, 1987, p. 60.

15. Ibid.

16. Waters, p. 54.

17. Personal interview with Dr. Alvin F. Poussaint, April 12, 1994.

18. Ibid.

Chapter 9

1. Bill Cosby, *Fatherhood* (New York: Doubleday Books, 1986), pp. 102–103.

2. Dan Goodgame and Bill Cosby, "I Do Believe in Control," *Time*, September 28, 1987, p. 56.

3. Bill Cosby, *Time Flies* (New York: Doubleday Books, 1987), p. 27.

4. Goodgame and Cosby, p. 56.

5. Nikki Finke, "Bill Cosby's Big Adventure," *Vanity Fair*, August 1993, p. 164.

6. Bob Thomas, "Cosby Talks," *Good Housekeeping*, February 1991, p. 216.

7. "Bill Cosby Pursues Joint Effort to Buy NBC Network," *Jet*, November 16, 1992, p. 55.

8. "Bill Cosby Stars in New Version of 'You Bet Your Life,'" *Jet*, October 26, 1992, p. 57.

9. Personal interview with Sheldon Leonard, March 15, 1994.

10. John J. O'Connor, "Comforts of Solving Comfortable Mysteries," *The New York Times*, October 19, 1994, p. C18.

11. Ibid.

12. "Cosby Condemns 'Massacre' of Black Images Depicted by 'Drive-By' White Writers," *Jet*, October 26, 1992, p. 59.

13. Harry F. Waters, "Cosby's Fast Track," *Newsweek*, September 2, 1985, p. 55.

14. Lisa Miller, "Tribute: Sheldon Leonard," *TV Guide*, February 1, 1997, p. 5.

15. Peter Johnson, "Cosby Admits to '70s Affair," *USA Today*, January 28, 1997, p. 1D.

16. Ibid.

17. Associated Press, "Cosby Admits to Affair with the Mother of Suspected Extortionist," *Keene Sentinel*, January 28, 1997, p. 6.

18. Associated Press, "Camille Cosby: Marriage Fine, Find My Son's Killer," *Keene Sentinel*, January 29, 1997, p. 14.

19. Deborah Sharp, "Composed Cosby Back Onstage," *USA Today*, February 3, 1997, p. 2D.

Further Reading

Adler, Bill. *The Cosby Wit: His Life and Humor.* New York: Carroll & Graf, 1986.

Bendicker, Jeanne, and Robert Bendicker. *Eureka! It's Television.* Brookfield, Conn.: Millbrook Press, 1993.

Blumenthal, Howard J. *Careers in Television.* Boston: Little Brown & Co., 1992.

Calabro, Marian. *Zap—A Brief History of Television.* New York: Four Winds Press, 1992.

Clemens, Virginia Phelps. *Behind the Filmmaking Scene.* Philadelphia: Westminster Press, 1982.

Cosby, Bill. *Fatherhood.* New York: Doubleday Books, 1986.

———. *Time Flies.* New York: Doubleday Books, 1987.

———. *Childhood.* New York: G.P. Putnam & Sons, 1991.

Schwartz, Perry. *Making Movies.* Minneapolis: Lerner Publications, 1989.

Twain, Mark. *The Adventures of Huckleberry Finn.* New York: Viking Penguin, 1986; or New York: Harper Collins, 1970.

Twain, Mark. *The Adventures of Tom Sawyer.* New York: Viking Penguin, 1986; or New York: Harper Collins, 1970.

Index

127